MW00813648

Expect Great Things,
Attempt Great Things

Expect Great Things, Attempt Great Things

William Carey and Adoniram Judson, Missionary Pioneers

EDITED BY
ALLEN YEH
AND
CHRIS CHUN

WITH A FOREWORD BY
DAVID BEBBINGTON

WIPF & STOCK · Eugene, Oregon

EXPECT GREAT THINGS, ATTEMPT GREAT THINGS
William Carey and Adoniram Judson, Missionary Pioneers

Copyright © 2013 Wipf and Stock Publishers. All rights reserved. Except for brief quotations in critical publications or reviews, no part of this book may be reproduced in any manner without prior written permission from the publisher. Write: Permissions, Wipf and Stock Publishers, 199 W. 8th Ave., Suite 3, Eugene, OR 97401.

Scripture quotations marked (NIV) are taken from the Holy Bible, New International Version®, NIV®. Copyright ©1973, 1978, 1984, 2011 by Biblica, Inc.™ Used by permission of Zondervan. All rights reserved worldwide.

Scripture quotations marked (KJV) are taken from the Holy Bible, King James Version, Cambridge, 1769.

Wipf & Stock
An Imprint of Wipf and Stock Publishers
199 W. 8th Ave., Suite 3
Eugene, OR 97401

www.wipfandstock.com

ISBN 13: 978-1-4982-6132-6

Manufactured in the U.S.A.

Dedicated to our students

Contents

Contributors | ix

Foreword by David Bebbington | xiii

Introduction by Allen Yeh and Chris Chun | xv

Part One: William Carey (1761–1834)

1   Let It Go: Lessons from the Life of William Carey | 3
    Timothy George

2   William Carey as a Missiologist: An Assessment | 15
    Timothy C. Tennent

3   Shoemaker and Missionary, William Carey: A *Dalit* Christian
    Perspective | 27
    Chakravarthy R. Zadda

4   Prophetic Precepts or Divine Preeminence? Rammohan Roy vs.
    Joshua Marshman on the Significance of Jesus | 42
    Sean Doyle

Part Two: Adoniram Judson (1788–1850)

5   Adoniram Judson and Orlando Costas: American Baptist Missions
    over Two Centuries | 63
    Allen Yeh

6   From the Judsons to Global Christianity, 1812–2012 | 74
    Todd M. Johnson

7   The Open and Hidden Legacy of Adoniram and Ann Judson:
    A Burmese Christian Woman's Perspective | 84
    May May Latt

8 George Liele: American Missions before Adoniram Judson | 93
  Soong-Chan Rah

Part Three: Two Great Mission Pioneers

9 "We Are Confirmed Baptists": The Judsons and Their Meeting with the Serampore Trio | 103
  Michael A. G. Haykin

10 Bloodlines and Bloodletting: Historic Themes in Baptist Missions | 113
  Jeff Iorg

11 The Sacrifices of Dorothy Carey and Ann Judson: Two Sides of the Same Coin | 125
  Chris Chun

  Index | 137

Contributors

David Bebbington (PhD, University of Cambridge) is professor of history at The University of Stirling. His publications include: *Evangelicalism in Modern Britain: A History from the 1730s to the 1980s*; *The Mind of Gladstone: Religion, Homer and Politics*; *The Dominance of Evangelicalism: The Age of Spurgeon and Moody*; *Baptists Through the Centuries: A History of a Global People*; and *Victorian Religious Revivals: Culture and Piety in Local and Global Contexts*.

Chris Chun (PhD, University of St. Andrews) is associate professor of church history at Golden Gate Baptist Theological Seminary near San Francisco, California. He is the author of *The Legacy of Jonathan Edwards in the Theology of Andrew Fuller* and has contributed chapters in *Jonathan Edwards in Scotland* and *Understanding Jonathan Edwards: An Introduction to America's Theologian*, as well as having been published in a variety of journals, including *The Southern Baptist Journal of Theology, American Baptist Quarterly, International Journal of Systematic Theology*, and *Church History and Religious Culture*.

Sean Doyle (PhD, University of Edinburgh) is associate professor of non-Western history at Geneva College in Beaver Falls, Pennsylvania. His research specialty is the history of Christian interaction with Hindu spirituality and philosophy. He is the author of the monograph *Synthesizing the Vedanta: The Theology of Pierre Johanns S. J.*

Timothy George (ThD, Harvard University) is the dean of Beeson Divinity School at Samford University in Birmingham, Alabama, and he serves as a member of *Christianity Today's* editorial council. A prolific author, he has written more than twenty books and regularly contributes to scholarly journals. His books include *Reading Scripture with the Reformers* and

Amazing Grace: God's Pursuit, Our Response. His *Theology of the Reformers* is the standard textbook on Reformation theology in many schools and seminaries and has been translated into multiple languages.

Michael A. G. Haykin (ThD, University of Toronto) is professor of church history and biblical spirituality at the Southern Baptist Theological Seminary in Louisville, Kentucky, where he also serves as the director of the Andrew Fuller Center for Baptist Studies. His main areas of research and writing are eighteenth-century Baptist life and thought and patristics. His publications include *Rediscovering the Church Fathers: Who They Were and How They Shaped the Church*; *Jonathan Edwards: The Holy Spirit in Revival*; *The Pure Fountain of the Word: Andrew Fuller as an Apologist*; *One Heart and One Soul: John Sutcliff of Olney, His Friends, and His Times*; and *The Spirit of God: The Exegesis of 1 and 2 Corinthians in the Pneumatomachian Controversy of the Fourth Century*.

Jeff Iorg (DMin, Southwestern Baptist Theological Seminary) is the president of Golden Gate Baptist Theological Seminary. Prior to his service at the seminary, he was the executive director of the Northwest Baptist Convention. Iorg teaches leadership, preaching, and church ministry courses at Golden Gate and his publications include *The Painful Side of Leadership*, *The Character of Leadership*, *Is God Calling Me?*, *The Case for Antioch*, and *Live Like a Missionary*, along with dozens of articles and curriculum materials.

Todd M. Johnson (PhD, William Carey International University) is associate professor of global Christianity and director of the Center for the Study of Global Christianity at Gordon-Conwell Theological Seminary. Johnson is visiting Research Fellow at Boston University's Institute for Culture, Religion and World Affairs leading a research project on international religious demography. He is coeditor of the *Atlas of Global Christianity* and coauthor of the *World Christian Encyclopedia* and *World Christian Trends*. He is co-editor of the *World Religion Database*.

May May Latt (PhD, Lutheran School of Theology at Chicago) is an adjunct lecturer at the Myanmar Institute of Theology. She is a native of Burma, also known as Myanmar. May May's publications include "Bible and Ecology: Genesis 2 and Current Issues," (in Burmese) in *Annual Magazine*, Myanmar Institute of Theology, September 2012. She wrote numerous essays, including "Women and Violence: Lessons Drawn from the Silence of Dinah in Genesis 34," (in Burmese) in *De Hlaing Than (The Sound of the Wave)*, August 2012, and "Life-Giving Women: Nurses and Midwives in the Bible (2 Kings 11 and Exodus 1)," (in Burmese) in *Women's Dawn Magazine*, Myanmar Institute of Theology, October 2012.

Soong-Chan Rah (DMin, Gordon-Conwell Theological Seminary) is Milton B. Engebretson associate professor of church growth and evangelism at North Park Theological Seminary in Chicago, Illinois. He is the author of *The Next Evangelicalism: Freeing the Church from Western Cultural Captivity* and *Many Colors: Cultural Intelligence for a Changing Church* and coeditor of *Honoring the Generations: Learning with Asian North American Congregations.*

Timothy C. Tennent (PhD, University of Edinburgh) is the president of Asbury Theological Seminary in Wilmore, Kentucky. He is the author of several books, including *Invitation to World Missions: A Trinitarian Missiology for the 21st Century*; *Theology in the Context of World Christianity*; and *Christianity at the Religious Roundtable.*

Allen Yeh (DPhil, University of Oxford) is associate professor of missiology and intercultural studies at Biola University near Los Angeles, California. He is the founder and chairman of the World Christianity consultation at the Evangelical Theological Society and serves on the International Ministries Board of Directors for the American Baptist Churches, USA. He is coauthor of *Routes and Radishes and Other Things to Talk About at the Evangelical Crossroads*, as well as a being a regular contributor to missiological journals such as the *International Bulletin of Missionary Research*, *International Journal of Frontier Missions*, and *Evangelical Missions Quarterly.*

Chakravarthy Zadda (PhD candidate, Lutheran School of Theology at Chicago) is a researcher in world Christianity and mission, specifically on Dalit Christian rights in India. He is the Danker Foundation Scholar and the Grover Wright Scholar at the Lutheran School of Theology at Chicago. As a Baptist pastor from India and an ordained minister in the American Baptist Churches (ABC) of Metro Chicago, Zadda is involved in empowering ethnic churches for issues of peace and justice in and around Chicago. He has lectured and taught courses in the area of missiology at several Baptist and Lutheran regional and national conferences organized by the ABC and Evangelical Lutheran Churches of America (ELCA). Zadda is presently serving as coordinator and chaplain for the international students at the Lutheran School of Theology at Chicago.

Foreword

In 1850, Jehu Lewis Shuck, a Baptist missionary serving under the auspices of the Southern Baptist Convention in Shanghai, wrote to Joseph Angus, secretary of the Baptist Missionary Society in London, telling him that the missionary presence in China had grown to seventy-five. Shuck, who had been the first American Baptist missionary to China, wanted the British organization to join in the evangelization of that land. "Some there are," he assured Angus, "who are praying in hope that the regular baptist churches of England may be able before a great while to start a mission at Shanghae [sic]."[1] Eight years previously, Shuck had managed to persuade the General Baptists of England to launch a mission to China, and now he was trying to induce the Particular Baptists, a much larger body with broadly Calvinist convictions, to do the same. His wishes were not to be fulfilled until 1859, after Shuck had returned to the United States. What is striking, however, is that, despite the already growing number of missionaries, the American wanted to augment them with people from Britain. In his eyes, the venture in which he was engaged was an Anglo-American cooperative enterprise. The missionary movement that gathered force during the nineteenth century was characteristically a joint effort of the two nations.

That is not to say that the whole foreign missionary impulse was confined exclusively to people of white, Anglo-Saxon stock. For one thing, missions had a long history before Britons or Americans became heavily involved around the opening of the nineteenth century. As *An Enquiry into the Obligation of Christians to Use Means for the Conversion of the Heathens* (1792), by William Carey, one of the main subjects of this book, points out, members of churches had preached the gospel to non-Christian peoples over long centuries. Carey notes, for example, that Roman Catholic missions had been sent out from countries on the European continent since the Reformation.

1. *Baptist Magazine*, November 1850, 689.

Another consideration is that, if we concentrate on Baptists alone, the first man who travelled abroad to spread the gospel was not white but a black ex-slave, George Liele. At the end of the American War of Independence, as chapter 8 in this book relates, Liele travelled with the defeated forces of the crown to Jamaica, establishing a flourishing series of black Baptist churches on the island. Yet Liele was American by birth and British by choice, and so he is rather less of an exception to the generalization about the Anglo-American nature of the missionary movement than he might appear. The most significant qualification of the generalization, however, lies in the role of indigenous peoples. Most of the work of spreading the gospel on the mission field was carried out not by expatriates but by local converts. Both Carey and Adoniram Judson, the other main individual discussed in these pages, encouraged preaching by people of the lands to which they travelled. The missions begun around 1800 formed a multiethnic undertaking from an early stage.

Nevertheless, the way in which early Baptist missionary efforts constituted a joint initiative by Britain and the United States is well illustrated by the pairing in this volume of Carey and Judson, an Englishman and an American. Carey was a visionary, a publicist and a versatile practitioner of mission in India; Judson was a resolute pioneer of the gospel in Burma. The two were bound together by mutual admiration. They met when Judson, having reached Baptistic convictions as he arrived in the East in 1812, was baptized by Carey's colleague William Ward. Carey's son Felix worked with Judson during his early years in Burma. So men of different nationalities were united in a common purpose. The charge has often been flung at overseas missions that they were a dimension of imperialism, a cultural aspect of national ambitions. The charge has been cogently answered,[2] but one reason for treating it with some skepticism is to appreciate that, at a time when Britain and America were actually at war, the two men were concerting their plans for the conversion of the East. They avowed a higher allegiance than their nations. Carey expressed the loyalties they both professed in the concluding sentence of his *Enquiry*. "Surely," he wrote, "it is worth while to lay ourselves out with all our might, in promoting the cause, and kingdom of Christ."[3]

—David Bebbington

2. See Brian Stanley, *The Bible and the Flag: Protestant Missions and British Imperialism in the Nineteenth and Twentieth Centuries* (Leicester, UK: Apollos, 1990); see also Andrew Porter, *Religion Versus Empire? British Protestant Missionaries and Overseas Expansion, 1700–1914* (Manchester: Manchester University Press, 2004).

3. William Carey, *An Enquiry into the Obligation of Christians to Use Means for the Conversion of the Heathens* (Leicester, UK: Ann Ireland, 1792), 87.

Introduction

WORLD CHRISTIANITY, THE SHIFT of the center of gravity of Christianity to the Two-Thirds World in the last half century, is a phenomenon that is increasingly coming to the attention and awareness of North Americans and Europeans. Christians in the West are surprisingly belated to realize this fact, and the secular media are even slower to grasp this reality. Nevertheless, in the last decade the scholarship on World Christianity has been steadily increasing. Despite this, there are still few scholars in this field beyond the usually-cited names of Andrew Walls, Lamin Sanneh, Dana Robert, Brian Stanley, Philip Jenkins, and a handful of others.

This volume attempts to redress several of the lacks cited above. The American Academy of Religion (AAR) started a World Christianity study group in 2006 at their annual meeting, which was held in Washington, DC, that year. The Evangelical Theological Society (ETS) did not have such a group, so the coeditors of this book, along with the others on the steering committee, took the initiative and started a World Christianity consultation at the ETS annual meeting in 2008, which was held in Atlanta that year, so as to raise the awareness of World Christianity among evangelical scholars.

This book is comprised of both accomplished scholars in the field, as well as emerging younger scholars, thus allowing for newer voices to join in the existing conversation and expanding the global scope of the book.

The 2011 ETS theme was "No Other Name," implying exclusivism and a missional emphasis, so the missionary pioneers William Carey (commonly known as the "Father of Modern Missions") and Adoniram Judson (often called "America's First Missionary") were chosen to be highlighted because of the 250th anniversary of Carey's birthday on August 17, 1761, and the 200th anniversary of Judson's mission departing the United States on February 19, 1812 and arriving in Burma on July 13, 1813. The second

ETS World Christianity consultation was held in San Francisco on November 17, 2011, which was situated right between these significant dates of Carey and Judson.

This present volume is unique because of several characteristics: (1) its World Christianity perspective, especially Indian and Burmese; (2) its Baptist perspective, since both William Carey and Adoniram Judson were Baptists; (3) its discussion of significant people related to Carey and Judson, such as their wives and the Serampore Trio; and 4) its parallel treatment of Carey and Judson. Some people think that the two are only tangentially related, but the case is being made here for a strong connection between the two. There have been many volumes written on Carey, and many on Judson, but this is the first to give them equal billing in a book.

There are three distinct divisions to this commemorative volume. Part 1 is dedicated to William Carey while part 2 is devoted to Adoniram Judson. Part 3 links these two missionary pioneers.

In chapter 1, the dean of Beeson Divinity School at Samford University and member of *Christianity Today* editorial council, Timothy George, paints William Carey as not only a missionary plodder, the champion of expecting great things and attempting great things, but also a significant "horizonal" figure in missions history, who stood at the "intersection of two epochs, between two times and yet oriented toward the future." Sometimes even at the risk of being accused of "harebrained schemes" by the standards of 1810, Carey's original vision of the modern ecumenical movement finally came into fruition in Edinburgh 1910.

In chapter 2, President of Asbury Theological Seminary, Timothy Tennent, assesses William Carey not only as a missionary practitioner but also as a missiologist by stepping back from Carey's specific contributions to examine his wider contribution. This chapter underscores how Carey departed from traditional ways of reading the Great Commission by emphasizing its missiological implications. He was a catalytic figure who challenged the "superior West inferior East" attitude of the Anglicists, as well as someone who redefined the missionary goals in terms of access and viability of the gospel. Tennent concludes that if not for Carey's contributions as a missiologist, it is unlikely that "the largest wave of missionary expansion in history" could have been accomplished.

In chapter 3, a unique contribution comes from Chakravarthy Zadda of southern India, currently at The Lutheran School of Theology at Chicago.

In the context of World Christianity, he presents not only an Indian but a *Dalit* (outcaste) perspective on William Carey. This biography, told from the vantage point of a different ethnicity, nationality, and social class than many Westerners are accustomed to, is a fresh take on a familiar figure. Seeing how an Indian regards Carey takes us beyond the theoretical to the practical: specifically, how one man continues to influence the religious, cultural, political, and social structures of this nation.

A history professor at Geneva College, Sean Doyle focuses chapter 4 on Carey's missionary colleague in Serampore, Joshua Marshman. By examining contours of the debates between Marshman and the Indian religious, social, and educational reformer Rammohan Roy, Doyle brings to light the evangelical Christological position of the Serampore Trio. This polemical dialogue provides a historical example of World Christianity, showing how an Indian scholar is able to engage in "high-level theological discussion, all the while using Christian sacred texts as sources of authority" in the nineteenth-century Anglo-Indian context.

In chapter 5, missions historian Allen Yeh of Biola University offers a comparative analysis of the lives of Adoniram Judson and Orlando Costas (1942–87), a Latino missiologist. Some of the similarities between these men are uncanny: Costas was commissioned for missions on the same famous settee that Judson was; Costas taught at Andover, where Judson attended school; the bicentennial of Judson's mission to Burma coincided with the annual Costas Global Mission Consultation of the Boston Theological Institute; and Judson was the missionary pioneer *par excellence* in the Great Century of Missions, just as Costas was a representative missiologist pioneer in this modern era of World Christianity.

In chapter 6, Todd Johnson of Gordon-Conwell Theological Seminary, a demographer by vocation, plies his trade by looking historically at Adoniram Judson and projecting missional trends into the future. Statistics are an illuminating perspective on the world and can offer a "forest" view of Christianity rather than just the "trees." Though there are obvious differences between the worlds of 1812 and 2012, the number of similarities may be surprising. Johnson provides a hopeful look at not only the challenges but the opportunities for missions, and connects the dots from early missionaries like the Judsons to the modern world of global Christianity.

It would not be fitting to have an Indian perspective on Carey without a Burmese perspective on Judson. In chapter 7, May May Latt, a Burmese woman who teaches at Myanmar Institute of Theology, tells of the contributions and legacy of Adoniram and Ann Judson to her country. She examines both the open and hidden legacies of this couple. Missions is not always an unqualified good, and Latt stresses not only the celebrated aspects of the Judsons but also the negative sides. Despite her reservations, however, she still acknowledges the positive influence of the Judsons in Burma.

In chapter 8, Soong-Chan Rah of North Park Seminary, and author of *The Next Evangelicalism*, focuses the modern thesis of his book on the past. Philip Jenkins's *The Next Christendom* states that the center of Christianity has shifted to the Two-Thirds World, but Rah applies that thesis domestically: the center of Christianity in the US has shifted to ethnic minorities and immigrants. Contrary to popular belief, Adoniram Judson was not the first overseas missionary from America; that distinction belongs to George Liele, a freed black slave who was a missionary to Jamaica thirty years before Judson set sail to Burma.

In chapter 9, Michael Haykin, a professor at the Southern Baptist Theological Seminary and general editor of the critical edition of *Works of Andrew Fuller*, highlights the cordial relationship that Adoniram and Ann Judson had with the Serampore Trio. The uniqueness of this chapter is to recount the period when Carey spent time with the Judsons, "talking with them, getting to know them well and praying with them." Carey's appraisal was that Judson was none other than "a man of God, one of the right stamp for missionary undertaking."

In chapter 10, Jeff Iorg, President of Golden Gate Baptist Theological Seminary, surveys characteristics of Baptist missions from its genesis to the present day. This chapter asserts that "characteristics and convictions" among the first Baptist missionaries, such as Carey and Judson, helped shape the denominational identity and later evolved into a source of conflict over missions-related issues. Since 1792, and for more than two hundred years, Iorg argues, the missionary enterprise has become part of the "bloodline" (who we are) as well as an "occasional bloodletting" (conflict) in Baptist history in general, and in the Southern Baptist heritage in particular.

Chris Chun, a church historian from Golden Gate Baptist Theological Seminary and coeditor of this book, writes a tribute in chapter 11 about the first wives of William Carey and Adoniram Judson. While Dorothy Carey and Ann Judson are polar opposites from one another, in other ways these two heroines are "two sides of the same coin," especially the way in which they sacrificed their lives. Chun makes a case that the successes of the husbands' historic ministries were largely due to Dorothy and Ann, who had laid the "sacrificial foundation" for them.

All told, this book proves that there is still a wealth of material to be mined about these two significant figures, and some two centuries later, William Carey and Adoniram Judson are still worthy to be remembered as relevant and significant to missions and World Christianity today. As the title of this volume indicates, these two historic missionary pioneers embodied the message that was the impetus for the nineteenth-century missionary movement: "Expect great things, Attempt great things."

—Coeditors

PART ONE

William Carey (1761–1834)

1

Let It Go

Lessons from the Life of William Carey

Timothy George

THERE HAVE BEEN MORE than fifty biographies of William Carey written since his death in 1834, which means that mine is only one of many. In light of the proliferation of works on the life of Carey, I am pleased that *Faithful Witness: The Life and Mission of William Carey*, originally published in 1991 on the 230th anniversary of Carey's birth, is now being translated into a number of languages throughout the world.[1]

Many of the biographies of Carey were produced in the nineteenth century. It was very common in that era to place Carey in a great line of notable individuals from English history. To quote George Smith, whose *The Life of William Carey* was published in 1885, these are

> Chaucer, the Father of English Verse; Wiclif [*sic*], the Father of the
> Evangelical Reformation in all lands; Hooker, the Father of English
> Prose; Shakspere [*sic*], the Father of English Literature; Milton, the
> Father of the English Epic; Bunyan, the Father of English Allegory;

1. Some of the content in this chapter is based on my biography on Carey, *Faithful Witness: The Life and Mission of William Carey* (Birmingham, AL: New Hope, 1991), as well as my essay, "Evangelical Revival and the Missionary Awakening," in *The Great Commission: Evangelicals and the History of World Missions*, ed. Martin I. Klauber and Scott M. Manetsch (Nashville: B&H, 2008), 45–63.

> Newton, the Father of English Science; Carey, the Father of the
> Second Reformation through Foreign Missions.[2]

Is that over the top? Is it too much to say something like that about a person whose humble beginnings included no more than a fifth- or sixth-grade education and who was almost completely self-taught? The answer becomes clear when we look at his life not from the beginning but from the end.

Carey died in 1834—the year that Charles Haddon Spurgeon was born—and by that time he had accomplished much. For example, he had become a Bible translator. In the tradition of the English reformer John Wycliffe, Carey, with the help of friends and pundits he met in India, personally translated the Bible not only into Bengali (the first language into which he translated the Scriptures), but eventually into twenty-eight other languages and dialects of India and the East, as well. From the press at Carey's institutions in Serampore there came forth forty-seven translations of the Scriptures into various languages in the East between the years of 1800 and 1834. In addition to the Bible, he also translated classic Hindu texts from the ancient language of Sanskrit.

Besides his legacy as a translator, Carey also became a social reformer. He worked for the abolition of *sati*, the ancient Indian funeral practice in which a widow would throw herself on her husband's pyre. He was also one of the first Protestant missionaries to protest abortion, the killing of preborn human beings. For his time, this was very unusual.

Carey was the founder of Serampore College, which today is a validating institution for all kinds of academic programs in India. He was also a journalist, the creator of newspapers and journals, and the founder of the first Indian agricultural society. We could go on for a long time reflecting on Carey's accomplishments. All things considered, then, perhaps the nineteenth-century hagiographical description of Carey as "the Father of the Second Reformation through Foreign Missions" is not far off the mark.

Such a designation dovetails nicely with Carey's other popularly ascribed title of "the Father of Modern Missions." Regardless of which appellation one uses, though, it is important to understand that they both signify Carey's role as the catalyst of rather than as the very first in modern missions. The Moravians, for example, of whom Carey was well aware, were doing missions well before him. They had produced a translation of the New Testament for Eskimos twenty years before Carey went to India. They

---

2. George Smith, *The Life of William Carey, D.D.: Shoemaker and Missionary* (London: John Murray, 1885), 439.

had already taken the gospel to Greenland and the West Indies, too, literally to "the uttermost parts of the earth."

Carey as catalyst essentially accomplished two things. For one, he provided that clarion call that resonated with so many people who had been praying and waiting expectantly for God's movement. The other accomplishment was his founding of a Christian community in Serampore. The story of Serampore was soon transmitted back to England and published in the periodicals and missions literature of that time. Carey's example inspired people like Henry Martyn to themselves go into the world with the good news of Jesus Christ. Carey's work at Serampore also inspired the 1795 founding of the London Missionary Society, an evangelical and interdenominational group.

William Carey has been described as a "path-breaker" or "pathfinder," and I think that is accurate. But I prefer another term: Carey was a "horizonal" figure. I don't mean "horizontal." Rather, I mean that he looked to the horizon. He was a figure who stood at the intersection of two epochs, between two times and yet oriented toward the future. This is why we must pay close attention to him and his many contributions to us.

Let us go back to the early development of Carey and ask these questions: What made him tick? What was his motivation? This is what interested me most in writing his biography.

Andrew Walls has said that "the modern missionary movement is an autumnal child of the Evangelical Revival."[3] I think this is true of William Carey and what he accomplished. In fact, the rise of the modern missionary movement among evangelicals in the Anglo-American world is often attributed to a sermon that Carey preached at Nottingham at the annual meeting of the Northampton Baptist Association on May 31, 1792.

He took as his text Isaiah 54:2-3. It is a fascinating text, presenting a picture of a woman who has lost her husband. She also has no children—she is "barren," in the language of the text. That means that she has no viable means of support. She is alone, isolated, detached from any kind of help in her hour of distress and need. And there she sits at the gates of Jerusalem, surrounded by desolation. The setting is that of the invasion of Jerusalem, during which the temple has been desecrated and there is no community to gather around her.

3. Andrew Walls, "The Evangelical Revival, the Missionary Movement, and Africa," in *Evangelicalism: Comparative Studies of Popular Protestantism in North America, the British Isles, and Beyond 1700–1900*, ed. Mark A. Noll et al. (New York: Oxford University Press, 1994), 310.

There is no support for her, and yet that Isaianic chapter begins with these amazing words that Carey picked up on in his sermon. God spoke to this woman, and he said to her, "Enlarge the place of your tent, stretch your tent curtains wide, do not hold back; lengthen your cords, strengthen your stakes. For you will spread out to the right and to the left; your descendants will dispossess nations and settle in their desolate cities" (Isaiah 54:2–3, NIV).

That is a remarkable statement for God to make to a widow—and to one who was in such dire circumstances at the moment. Carey picked up on this language that God used on this occasion, and he said to his fellow ministers, "What God said to that woman, he is saying to us! In some ways, we are like this woman. We have no resources; we are destitute. We cannot do very much, and yet God is saying to us just what he said to her: 'Stretch forth your tent curtains wide.' Start a building program. Expand!"

Carey was also breaking new ground in the way he applied the Great Commission of Matthew 28:19–20. In orthodox churches at the time, the prevailing sentiment was that the Great Commission was no longer in effect. It was meant for the apostles, most believed, and they had fulfilled it long ago. But Carey believed otherwise. Consistent with his horizonal character, he believed that the Great Commission still applied in his day. When he read it, he thought to himself, "'Go ye' means me! It means you! Here and now!" So he began to talk about the Great Commission not as a historical descriptor but as a direct imperative from the risen Christ to the churches of his own day.

Carey summarized his famous sermon in those words that John Clifford once called "two plain, practical, pungent, quotable watchwords." Carey said, "Expect great things. Attempt great things." Later in the nineteenth century, those who wrote about Carey expanded that statement into the one more familiar to us today: "Expect great things from God. Attempt great things for God." It is debatable whether Carey ever added "for God" and "from God." I do not think he needed to. What is really important is the sequence. The *expectation* came before the *attempt*! Carey's own God-intoxicated theology was motivating him to make such a challenge to those backwater Baptists in the middle of England, people who had virtually no resources and no connections.

Later, Carey went to London and tried to get support for his mission from the bigwig Baptists in the denomination, but they were not interested in him. They had not heard about him. They thought that his mission was a fanciful idea that most likely would come to nothing. But none of this could dampen the enthusiasm Carey had for the challenge that was before him.

In rising to meet the challenge of taking the gospel to the world and renewing the call for others to do likewise, Carey was well aware of the legacy of Christian missions. Like the Great Commission, the legacy of missions was largely unknown or underappreciated by orthodox Christians at the time. Carey, though, was a student of the history of Christian missions. He could trace missions all the way through the history of the church. He knew, for example, about Patrick in Ireland, the medieval missionaries among the Slavs, and the Moravians, whom Carey regarded as exemplary in their missionary activities. Carey even used the Moravians to cajole and shame his fellow Baptists, essentially saying, "Look at what the Moravians are doing. If they can do this with so little means, why can't the Baptists? Why must we be outliers?"

Carey's great sermon at Nottingham was only one of several calls to missionary action during the period. For example, Thomas Coke, the indomitable juggernaut of Methodist missions, had already published his *A Plan of the Society for the Establishment of Missions among the Heathen* in 1783. That was the year in which Carey himself was baptized as a Baptist Christian. Another example is from the Anglican world: David Brown, who had been a chaplain appointed by the East India Company, and Charles Grant, one of the chaplain's officials, issued *A Proposal for Establishing a Protestant Mission in Bengal and Bihar* in 1787.

Carey built upon these previous works and others like them. However, Carey's talk about expectation—"Expect great things"—tapped into a deeper impulse stemming from the earlier revivals. This was true not only of the Wesleyan revival in England but also spiritual stirrings in North America.

Here I think we have to note two books by Jonathan Edwards that had a profound influence not only on Carey but on the whole missionary awakening at the end of the eighteenth century and the beginning of the nineteenth century. The first of these was the diary of David Brainerd, who had been engaged to Edwards's daughter but died quite prematurely. Edwards published Brainerd's diary in 1749 as *An Account of the Life of the Late Reverend Mr. David Brainerd*. It is hard to overemphasize the influence of this publication on those who took up the missionary cause in subsequent generations. This was one of the few books that Carey took with him on board the Danish ship *Kron Princess Maria*, which carried him on that five-month voyage from England to India. Carey read Brainerd's diary day after day. He became so familiar with it that he knew it by heart. In a sense, Carey relived, in his own context, the experience of Brainerd.

He was not the only one to do so. Henry Martyn, a disciple of Charles Simeon and friend of Carey, who became a great missionary to Persia, also was inspired by Brainerd. Concerning Brainerd's diary, Martyn said, "I read David Brainerd today and yesterday and found as usual my spirit greatly benefited by it. I longed to be like him. Let me forget the world and be swallowed up in a desire to glorify God." On another occasion, Martyn likewise said, "Read Brainerd. I feel my heart knit to this dear man and really rejoice to think of meeting him in heaven."[4]

The other Jonathan Edwards book that had a profound impact on Carey's calling and vocation as a missionary to India was *An Humble Attempt to Promote an Explicit Agreement and Visible Union of God's People Through the World, in Extraordinary Prayer, for the Revival of Religion, and the Advancement of Christ's Kingdom on Earth, Pursuant to Scripture-promises and Prophecies Concerning the Last Time*. This was essentially a call to prayer. It was written with the early evangelical awakening surrounding the John Erskine movement in Scotland in mind. For a number of years, though, it apparently was forgotten, until a Baptist pastor who lived in Carey's area, John Sutcliff, brought it back up.

Sutcliff is a relatively unknown hero in this story, one who needs to be much more widely known than he is. While writing to a friend in Scotland, Sutcliff essentially said, "We Baptists are poor down here. We do not have any money. Could you please send us some good books?" So his friend packed up a packet of books and sent them to Sutcliff. Among them was Edwards's work *An Humble Attempt*. Sutcliff read this book, and it lit a fire in his soul. He said, "We've got to do this, too! We cannot just rely on our Scottish brothers of the previous generation in praying to God." So Sutcliff and his associates began a concert of prayer among the local churches.

They began to pray for a revival in England, meaning that at first they were not praying for a great missionary revival around the world. But in the course of ten years of a sustained concert of prayer, something happened in their hearts—their vision was expanded. They began to understand that what they wanted God to do in their churches was something that God wanted to happen elsewhere, too—and they might be the divinely ordained means to use to that end. All of this was leading up to Sutcliff's

---

4. Constance E. Padwick, *Henry Martyn: Confessor of the Faith* (London: Inter-Varsity Fellowship, 1953), 49.

great missionary call, which I think could not have taken place without the influence of Edwards.

Sutcliff did not agree with every aspect of Edwards's eschatology, but he did share a sense that was widespread among his generation, Carey included, that they were indeed living on the very edge of the consummation of time. For his part, Carey had preached a series of weekly sermons on the book of Revelation during his pastorate in Leicester just prior to his departure for India. The end times were very much on his mind and on his heart as he prepared to leave for India.

Sutcliff, after reading Edwards's book, projected that there would be a gradual advance of the gospel that, if carried out with amazing and unparalleled progress, could conceivably usher in the millennium by the year AD 2000. Specifically, according to his projection, the purity of the church would be restored among the Protestants in the half century between 1750 and 1800, the Roman Catholics would come to the full light of evangelical truth from 1800 to 1850, the Muslim world and the Jewish world would be converted between 1850 and 1900, and during the twentieth century the whole world would be enlightened and come to accept the Christian faith. Then all things would be set so that the whole world in the year 2000 would move into what Edwards called "a holy rest, or sabbatism."[5] We recognize this as a kind of postmillennial eschatology that was very much part of the Great Awakening movement. I think it gave a kind of edge to those who went out—an edge based upon expectation. Remember what Carey said: "Expect great things!"

An Enquiry into the Obligations of Christians to Use Means for the Conversion of the Heathens[6] was Carey's one great work, apart from his diary and his letters. We do not have a lot of the journal or newspaper articles that he wrote while in India. We do not have a lot of lengthy works from Carey. He was a doer—an activist—more than a writer.

And yet this one little book, *An Enquiry*, is itself a remarkable document. It is worth reading because in many ways it is a kind of horizonal book—it looks to the future. For example, one of the things Carey did with it was survey the world. He conducted something of a statistical study, asking, "How many people live here? What is the climate there? What is the basis of economy there?" The kinds of things that we have come to know

---

5. Jonathan Edwards, *The Works of Jonathan Edwards*, ed. Edward Hickman (Edinburgh: Banner of Truth Trust, 1974), 1:306.

6. Published Leicester, UK: Ann Ireland, 1792.

and appreciate in the *World Christian Encyclopedia* can actually be found in Carey's *An Enquiry*, which he himself was able to bring together through his own hard work.

Gathering in Sutcliff's church in Olney, Carey and the others who were to leave in 1793 were commissioned. They sang a closing hymn that resounded with lyrics that were characteristic of Carey and the kind of sacrifice that he was willing to make:

> And must I part with all I have,
> Jesus, my Lord, for Thee?
> This is my joy, since Thou hast done
> Much more than this for me.
> Yes, let it go: one look from thee
> Will more than make amends
> For all the losses I sustain,
> Of credits, riches, friends.[7]

At the conclusion of the service, Carey then famously said to his friends, "I will go but remember that you must hold the ropes."[8]

I think that four simple words in the lyrics just cited are a summary of Carey's life, his devotion, and the motivation that led him to leave his home country, to never return to England, and to live with the people of India for more than forty years. "Yes, let it go," they sang. Carey indeed let it all go in order to follow the Great Commission call of his Lord.

Carey learned many languages while in India. He learned not only Bengali, which was the language of the masses in India, but he also took pains to learn Sanskrit. This was a somewhat controversial decision that he made. I have been told by those who should know that it is a very difficult language, particularly for someone from the West, to learn and master. Carey nonetheless published a Sanskrit dictionary and grammar, as well as a translation of the New Testament in Sanskrit. All of this work was in addition to bringing out critical editions of the great Hindu epics, long poems in the tradition of Homer's *Iliad* and *Odyssey*.

Back in England, when Carey's dear friend and supporter Andrew Fuller found out about what Carey had been doing, spending all his time

---

7. Leighton Williams and Mornay Williams, eds., *Serampore Letters: Being the Unpublished Correspondence of William Carey and Others with John Williams, 1800–1816* (New York: G. P. Putnam's Sons, 1892), 12.

8. F. A. Cox, *History of the Baptist Missionary Society, from 1792 to 1842* (London: T. Ward and G. & J. Dyer, 1842), 1:120.

on these Hindu translations, he wondered whether Carey was wasting his time. In the face of these suggestions, Carey responded, saying that he had three reasons for doing so. First, he felt that he could not adequately counter the arguments of the Brahmins unless he knew firsthand their own Scriptures. Second, by mastering these writings, he was better able to translate the Bible into Sanskrit, and so offer a positive witness to the gospel. Finally, there was an economic motive.

For the most part, Carey and the mission at Serampore were on their own. There was great conflict between the Baptist Missionary Society in England and the mission at Serampore, which meant that they were largely dependent on their own resources to make things work. At the same time, there was a market for Sanskrit texts, and their publication would prove profitable for the mission. So Carey was willing to spend his time delving into these mysterious sacred texts of ancient Hindu writings in order to provide revenue for the publication of Christian Scriptures and the propagation of the true gospel.

While in India, Carey showed himself once again as a horizonal figure in his efforts to bring various denominations together for the sake of advancing the gospel through missions. Having realized the need to work with the Anglicans and, later, Methodists, General Baptists, and Presbyterians, he made this famous appeal:

> Would it not be possible to have a general association of all denominations of Christians, from the four corners of the world, held there once in about ten years? I earnestly recommend this plan, that the first meeting be in the year 1810, or 1812 at furthest. I have no doubt but it would be attended with many important effects. We could understand one another better, and more entirely enter into one another's views by two hours' conversation than by two or three years of epistolary correspondence.[9]

Unfortunately for Carey, Fuller and his associates back in England had no interest in this. It was another one of his harebrained schemes, they said, so there was not to be a "general association of all denominations of Christians" in 1810, in 1812, or at any point in Carey's lifetime. It would not be until 1910 that such a worldwide meeting finally took place in Edinburgh,

9. Carey to Andrew Fuller, Calcutta, 15 May 1806, cited by Kenneth Scott Latourette, "Ecumenical Bearings of the Missionary Movement and the International Missionary Council," in *A History of the Ecumenical Movement: 1517–1948*, ed. Ruth Rouse and Stephen Charles Neill (Geneva: World Council of Churches, 1954), 355n2.

but the seeds of the modern quest for Christian unity had been born on the mission field, springing from Carey and fellow Bible-believing Christians who held to the possibility of unity among members of the Body of Christ for the sake of evangelization.

Carey was sometimes called an "enthusiast," which was considered a putdown in the eighteenth century because it meant that someone was fanatical and unbalanced, but in actuality he had a very practical mind. He later said,

> If, after my removal, anyone should think it worth his while to write my life, I will give you a criterion by which you may judge of its correctness. If he gives me credit for being a plodder, he will describe me justly. Anything beyond this will be too much. I can plod. I can persevere in any definite pursuit.[10]

Carey was referring to his early days as a shoemaker, working with the leather, figuring out how much the boots were going to cost, taking them to the market in town—all of this kind of business. Practical sense was very much part of the Serampore community and Carey's work as the leader of it.

In closing, I want to say a few words about Carey's theology. If there is one contribution that I might have made in writing my biography of Carey, one that a lot of the other biographers skimp on or skip over altogether, it is that I gave quite a bit of attention to the theology of missions that was at the heart of Carey's call and his venture to India.

Back in the 1920s and 1930s, there arose a certain expression in ecumenical missions circles: "Theology divides, missions unites." The idea behind the saying was that people ought not to get much involved in theology. Instead, what they should focus on is the practical ministry of missions and working together and doing good things in the name of Christ. They wanted to just forget about theology. Such a saying, however, represents a very shallow understanding of the real motivation of missions. Carey certainly went to India imbued with a sense of the reality of God and God's call, not only on his life but on the church, as well.

There were two branches of Baptists in England in Carey's day: the General Baptists, who had by and large been swallowed up in Arianism and even Unitarianism by the time Carey came on the scene in 1791, and the Particular Baptists, also known as the Calvinistic Baptists. The Calvinistic Baptists had become rather hardened in some of their views, to the point

---

10. Quoted in Smith, *Life*, vii.

that there was no promiscuous preaching of the gospel; there was no open offer of the gospel. Carey, though, came on the scene and was able to accept and build upon a new theology of missions that had emerged from his friend Fuller. We might call it a kind of evangelical Calvinism. (The General Baptists, led by Daniel Taylor, also experienced a renewal of this sort in the same period.) One consequence of the rise of evangelical Calvinism was that there came about a Particular Baptist Missionary Society, which followed in the tradition of the Calvinistic Baptists.

This evangelical Calvinism spawned by Fuller emphasized a couple of words that could be found in the title of Carey's *An Enquiry*. One was "obligation," and the other was "means." The connection between the premise of evangelical Calvinism and Carey's seminal work was an argument that went like this: If sinners were obliged to repent and believe in Christ, as the Bible makes clear they are, was there not another obligation to be considered? Were not Christians, who themselves had been delivered from darkness into light, more urgently obliged to present the claims of Jesus Christ to those who had never heard? As the Baptist leader Robert Hall put it: "The way to Jesus is graciously open to anyone who chooses to come to Him."[11] The God who predestined the salvation of the elect also predestined the means by which they would be saved. And the means that God had chosen included the sending of the missionaries, the raising up of evangelists, and the preaching of the gospel to all persons everywhere without exception.

Wesleyans were very much also into this kind of Great Commission theology, although they argued it from a slightly different theological basis. That being said, the point I want to make about Carey and his theology is this: the doctrinal wars over predestination could be divisive and ill-tempered and destructive of Christian fellowship, but, faced with the challenge of world evangelization, missionary leaders on both sides of this theological divide frequently found a way to collaborate in prayer, in works of benevolence, and in evangelism for the sake of sharing the gospel with the lost. Many evangelical Calvinists could appreciate Wesley's strong doctrine of original sin, objective atonement, and justification by faith alone. On the other side, most evangelical Methodists could resonate with George Whitefield's maxim that "every man's damnation is of himself and every

---

11. Robert Hall, *Help to Zion's Travellers: Being an Attempt to Remove Various Stumbling Blocks out of the Way, Relating to Doctrinal, Experimental and Practical Religion* (London: Whittingham & Rowland, 1815), 103.

man's salvation is all of God."[12] Carey was a model of this collaborative spirit while living and ministering in India.

Carey died in Serampore at age 72. What was once a horizonal life has long since become a horizonal legacy. "Expect great things, attempt great things"—this phrase continues to stir the hearts of many to missionary service. The Great Commission continues to be understood as an ongoing directive of the Lord Jesus Christ. And believers continue to "let it go," leaving behind the life they have known to participate in the worldwide evangelistic movement of the Holy Spirit of God. Carey has become part of the very legacy of Christian missions that he once, as a humble cobbler, studied and wrote about in order to cajole his fellow Baptists into action.

12. Quoted in Stuart Piggin, *Making Evangelical Missionaries, 1789–1858* (London: Sutton Courtenay, 1984), 93.

2

William Carey as a Missiologist

An Assessment

Timothy C. Tennent

INTRODUCTION

THE PURPOSE OF THIS chapter is to examine William Carey as a missiologist, not as a missionary. Much has been written of Carey's contribution as a missionary, and he is widely regarded as the father of the modern, Protestant missionary movement. This chapter will not attempt to survey the life or contributions of Carey, as that has been done in many notable articles and books.[1] This chapter seeks to step back from the many *specific* contributions of Carey and look at his *wider* contribution as a missiologist.

Missiology, or the study of missions, has only in the modern period been recognized as a separate discipline within the theological community. Traditionally, theological studies have fallen into four separate areas known as the "fourfold pattern": the disciplines of the Bible (text), church history

1. The standard biography of Carey remains S. Pearce Carey, *William Carey, D.D.: Fellow of Linnaean Society* (London: Carey Press, 1934). One of the best contemporary biographical works is Timothy George, *Faithful Witness: The Life and Mission of William Carey* (Birmingham, AL: New Hope, 1991). For a more comprehensive view of the history of Baptist Missions in Serampore, see the excellent work by E. Daniel Potts, *British Baptist Missionaries in India, 1793-1937: The History of Serampore and Its Missions* (London: Cambridge University Press, 1967).

(history), systematic theology (truth), and practical theology (application).[2] Under the influence of Schleiermacher, this pattern became normative in Protestant theological education throughout North America. Missiology, if it was taught at all, had to be related to one of these four areas. Many schools appended missiology to practical theology, others to church history. However, as the missionary movement expanded in the nineteenth and twentieth centuries and began to raise many new issues and challenges, it became increasingly difficult to relate missiology to one of the four traditional disciplines. Thus, in 1867 the Alexander Duff Chair of Evangelistic Theology was established in Edinburgh and for the first time "missiology was taught as an independent subject in its own right."[3] Later in the early twentieth century, due to the efforts of Gustav Warneck at the University of Halle, missiology began to be more generally liberated from its ancillary status and emerged into the full light of acceptance as a separate discipline. It is therefore with some admitted anachronism that this attempt is being made to look back on Carey and assess his significance as a missiologist. However, this makes Carey's contributions as a missiologist even more remarkable.

There are at least three areas where Carey demonstrates remarkable foresight as a missiologist and should, therefore, be regarded not only as a pioneer missionary, but also as a leading missiologist in his own right. Each of the three areas highlighted continues to instruct and inform the church today as we reflect upon the "apostolate" aspect of the church's mission in the world.

CAREY AND THE GREAT COMMISSION

First, William Carey's understanding of the "Great Commission" was a radical break from the history of interpretation of the passage from the Patristics through the Reformation.

William Carey made a radical departure from the traditional ways in which the Great Commission, especially as found in Matthew 28:18–20, was understood—not only by his contemporaries but by many throughout church history, including the Protestant Reformers. There is a general amazement in the faces of most modern-day evangelicals when they discover that Matthew 28:18–20 was only rarely viewed as a missions text

---

2. See David J. Bosch, *Transforming Mission: Paradigm Shifts in Theology of Mission* (Maryknoll, NY: Orbis, 1991), 490.

3. Bosch, *Transforming*, 491.

through much of church history. However, a study of the history of the interpretation of the passage demonstrates that the two most frequent ways the passage was used were either to support the deity of Christ or to support a Trinitarian baptismal formula. During the Arian controversy in the fourth century, the text was frequently used to demonstrate the coequal status of Jesus Christ with God the Father.[4] The other major use of the passage is exemplified by Tertullian's use of the passage to emphasize the importance of the Trinitarian baptismal formula. Tertullian, commenting on Matthew 28:18–20, says, "For the law of baptism has been imposed and the formula prescribed, 'Go, teach the nations, baptizing them in the name of the Father, and of the Son and of the Holy Spirit.'"[5] This dual emphasis on Matthew 28:18–20 as a text to support the deity of Christ and a text that teaches the proper baptismal formula continued through the Reformation, and the passage was only seldom used in a missiological context.[6]

The seeming inability of the Reformers to embrace a global expansion of the gospel based on Matthew 28:18–20 is generally attributed to two main causes. First, the Reformers believed that the missional aspect of the passage had already been fulfilled by the original apostles, and therefore that dimension of the passage simply did not apply to the church in succeeding generations. It was, to use the language of the Theological Faculty of Wittenberg in 1651 when asked for their view on this subject, the *personale privilegium* of the apostles.[7] Second, the Reformers were hampered

---

4. Abraham Friesen, *Erasmus, the Anabaptists, and the Great Commission* (Grand Rapids: Eerdmans, 1998), 117.

5. Alexander Roberts, et al., eds, *Ante-Nicene Fathers*, vol. 3, *Latin Christianity: Its Founder, Tertullian* (Grand Rapids: Eerdmans, 1998), 676.

6. The most notable exception was Erasmus. For an excellent discussion of Erasmus's views and his influence on the later Anabaptist "non-territorial" views on missions, see Friesen, *Erasmus*.

7. See Ronald E. Davies, "The Great Commission from Calvin to Carey," *Evangel* 14, no. 2 (1996) 45, online: http://www.biblicalstudies.org.uk/pdf/evangel/14-2_davies.pdf. According to Davies, the famous Wittenberg "Opinion" also underscored the Reformers' belief that "nobody could be excused before God by reason of ignorance, because God has revealed himself to all people through nature as well as *through the preaching of the apostles*" (italics added). See also Bosch, *Transforming*, 251–52. The view that the Great Commission had already been fulfilled in the Apostolic Age was, according to Bosch, emphatically taught by Johann Gerhard (1582–1637) and Philipp Nicolai (1556–1608) and was generally held by the Reformers. See also Nicolai, *De Regno Christi* (1596), in which Nicolai develops his "geography of missions." For Luther's views, see "Gospel Sermon, Second Sunday after Easter" and "Gospel Sermon, Ascension Day," in *Luther's Works*, ed. J. N. Lenker (Minneapolis: Lutherans in All Lands, 1907), 12:25–26, 183–84.

by a territorial view of Christianity that did not permit the spreading of the gospel in areas not governed by a Christian ruler. David Bosch, in *Transforming Mission*, summarizes the dominant view well when he states that "the Reformers could not conceive of a missionary outreach into countries in which there was no Protestant government."[8] The principle in Europe after the Reformation was *cuius regio, eius religio* (each region has to follow the religion of its ruler). Catholicism would be the established religion in Catholic countries, Lutheranism in Lutheran territories, and so forth. The precedent for this as a missiological principle had been set as far back as Pope Alexander VI (1431–1503), known not only for his patronage of Michaelangelo's *Pietà*, but, more significantly, the issuance of a papal bull in 1493 (*Inter Caetera Divinae*), which divided the outside of Europe between the kings of Portugal and Spain. It became known as the "patronage" principle (*padroado* in Portuguese) and was adopted by the Reformers. In short, it affirmed that the ruler of a given dominion had authority over a colony both politically and ecclesiastically. This territorial view of Christian expansion lay at the root of the division between the magisterial Reformers and the Anabaptists. Abraham Friesen observes, "The earth, said the Anabaptists, did not belong to the temporal rulers, nor even to the established churches. It belonged to Christ and he had commanded his followers to proclaim his teachings."[9] The "wandering" of the Anabaptist evangelists was widely condemned by the Reformers.

The birth of Protestant missions further illustrates this point. The Danish King Frederick IV's justification for sending out the first Protestant missionaries to India, Bartholomew Ziegenbalg and Henry Plutschau, was that he was the temporal ruler of the Indian colony of Tranquebar and therefore had the responsibility and right to propagate the gospel in that particular realm. The Royal Danish Mission, which sent out Ziegenbalg and Plutschau in 1705, was clearly rooted in territorial views of Christian expansion.

With this background, it is now possible to see how William Carey not only represents a radical departure from how the text had been understood historically, but, more significantly, a break from the mainstream Protestant

---

Luther and Calvin both believed that the Great Commission had already been fulfilled during the Apostolic Age. This view, however, was not held by Augustine, who wrote that "in Africa there are innumerable barbarian tribes to whom the gospel has not yet been preached." Maurice Wiles and Mark Santer, eds, *Documents in Early Christian Thought* (Cambridge: Cambridge University Press, 1975), 259–60.

8. Bosch, *Transforming*, 246.

9. Friesen, *Erasmus*, 99.

perspective on missions since the time of the Reformation. Carey insisted that the Great Commission had not been fulfilled and that the contemporary church remained bound to it. Carey acknowledged the prevailing view of his time when he wrote:

> There seems to be an opinion existing in the minds of some, that because the Apostles were extraordinary officers and have no proper successors, and because many things that were right for them to do would be utterly unwarrantable for us, therefore it may not be immediately binding on us to execute the commission, though it was so upon them.[10]

Carey then proceeds to argue convincingly that if the Great Commission is no longer binding, then Christians also have no warrant to baptize, nor any assurance of his divine presence that was assured "to the end of the age," since these are all components of the same text.[11] Carey reminds us that since Paul and Silas were forbidden by the Holy Spirit to preach the word in the province of Asia and in Bithynia (Acts 16:6–7) and there were many islands in the South Sea that were impossible for the apostles to reach, it is indefensible to argue that the whole inhabitable globe was reached by the apostles.[12] He also attacked the territorial notion of Christian expansion that continued to be held in his day. Carey pointed out that "this commission was as extensive as possible, and laid them under obligation to disperse themselves into every country of the inhabitable globe, and preach to all the inhabitants, without exception or limitation."[13] He was convinced that simply on the authority of Christ we have the responsibility to form missionary societies that focus exclusively on mobilizing the church to bring the gospel to the unreached world. In Nottingham, on May 31, 1792, Carey preached his famous "Expect great things, attempt great things" sermon based on Isaiah 54:3. When, at the end of the meeting, everyone

10. William Carey, *An Enquiry into the Obligations of Christians to Use Means for the Conversion of the Heathens* (London: Baptist Missionary Society, 1934), 8. See also Francis M. DuBose, ed., *Classics of Christian Missions* (Nashville: Broadman, 1979), 26.

11. Carey was accurate in his exegesis since the passage only contains one imperative, the verb "make disciples," whereas the other three supporting participles, "going," "baptizing," and "teaching," all carry equal weight in the passage. Carey's argument in *An Enquiry* had been articulated earlier by the Dutch Reformer Adrian Saravia (1531–1613) in *De diversis ministrorum evangelii gradibus, sicut a Domino fuerunt instituti*, written in 1590. However, Saravia's views were not widely accepted.

12. Carey, *Enquiry*, 10.

13. DuBose, *Classics*, 26.

was leaving, Carey spoke to Andrew Fuller, the great Baptist theologian, gripping his arm, saying, "Are you, after all, again going to do nothing?"[14] Within six months the first Baptist Society was formed, on October 2, 1792, for the purpose of "propagating the gospel among the Heathen." Through this agency "Carey projected the first organization in England for missions to the human race outside of Christendom."[15] Carey's vision for missionary societies soon became a radical new model of ecclesiology—an *ecclesiola in ecclesia* that organized the church for mission on the sole authority of Christ's Commission without any reference to secular authority.[16]

In Carey's famous sermon, "expect great things" memorably preceded the phrase "attempt great things." This clearly roots Carey's missiology in the *missio Dei*, in marked contrast to today's missiology, which almost inevitably begins with our attempts and then prays expectantly for God to bless the work of our hands. Carey wisely understood that missions appropriately begins with our expectation of God to act prior to our plans or actions. Yet, Carey goes on to entitle his landmark document *An Enquiry into Obligations of Christians to Use Means for the Conversion of the Heathens,* etc. The phrase "to use means" in the title of his famous *Enquiry* demonstrates Carey's remarkable ability to move from the *missio Dei* to a positive plan of action in setting up a Protestant sodality in the form of a mission society. The Roman Catholics had sustained their global missionary effort through an extensive use of sodality structures, but this had been lost in the Reformation. Carey, whose only pattern was the East India secular trading society, gave birth to a sodality structure that would end up fueling the entire "Great Century" of Protestant missions.

CAREY THE ORIENTALIST

Second, Carey was an Orientalist, not an Anglicist.

The nineteenth century represents the high-water mark of the British colonial empire. Administratively, Britain adopted an Anglicist policy

14. Mark Galli, "The Man Who Wouldn't Give Up," *Christian History* 36, October 1, 1992.

15. J. T. K. Daniel and R. E. Hedlund, eds., *Carey's Obligation and India's Renaissance* (Serampore College, 1993), 104.

16. An "ecclesiola in ecclesia" means, broadly, a "church within a church." The expression is used to denote church movements that take place within the larger structure of the church.

toward India as a pragmatic way to govern. It was considered prudent to teach enough natives the English language to effectively govern and to disseminate Western thought into the Indian context. This policy tended to promote ethnocentric attitudes among the British working in India, and this affected traders, colonialists, and missionaries. Thomas Babington Macaulay was appointed by the British Parliament to direct the diffusion of the English language into India. Macaulay openly admitted that he had "no knowledge of either Sanskrit or Arabic," yet he wrote that "all the books written in the Sanskrit language are less valuable than what may be found in the most paltry abridgements used at preparatory schools in England."[17] After the Charter Act of 1813 lifted the ban on missionary activities in India, dozens of missionaries entered India as English teachers. Sir Charles Wood, the British Secretary of State, issued a dispatch in 1854 that dramatically increased the funding and involvement of Britain in English education in India. The aim was to train reliable civil servants, promote efficiency, and diffuse European ideals throughout the subcontinent. Wood states the following in the Dispatch of 1854:

> We must emphatically declare that the education which we desire to see extended in India is that which has for its object the diffusion of the improved arts, science, philosophy and literature of Europe; in short, of European knowledge. . . . We look, therefore, to the English language and to the vernacular languages of India together as the media for the diffusion of European knowledge.[18]

By 1885, the British government had either established or given financial assistance to 1,474 schools and Christian missionaries had established or maintained 1,628 schools.

The Anglicists generally embraced a "superior West, inferior East" attitude. They tended to emphasize the vast differences between the East and

17. Stanley A. Wolpert, *A New History of India* (Oxford: Oxford University Press, 1993), 215.

18. Tara Chand, *History of the Freedom Movement in India* (Delhi: Ministry of Information and Broadcasting, 1967), 2:205. Macaulay's 1835 Minute on Education is most revealing. He stated concerning the 1813 Act that "we are not fettered by any pledge expressed or implied; that we are free to employ our funds as we choose; that we ought to employ them in teaching what is best worth knowing; that English is better worth knowing than Sanskrit or Arabic I feel with them, that it is impossible for us, with our limited means, to attempt to educate the body of the people. We must at present do our best to form a class who may be interpreters between us and the millions whom we govern; a class of persons, Indian in blood and colour, but English in taste, in opinions, in morals and in intellect." B. N. Pandey, *A Book of India* (Calcutta: Rupa, 1991), 62–63.

the West, not indigenous points of contact. As noted above, this attitude influenced many of the missionaries who came to India. Alexander Duff, the famous Scottish missionary to India, is an example of a well-known missionary who was also a thoroughgoing Anglicist. Duff did not utilize the indigenous languages. Duff's vision was to focus on giving the influential, upper castes of India an English education. He was convinced that English-based education was the key to the disintegration of Hinduism. Defending his ministry to the General Assembly of the Church of Scotland in 1835, Duff declared, "The English language, I repeat it, is the lever which, as the instrument of conveying the entire range of knowledge, is destined to move all of Hindustan."[19] Duff was convinced, therefore, that the establishment of English schools and colleges was essential to the propagation of Christianity in India, and ultimately, the undermining of Hinduism. In the same address to the General Assembly, Duff insisted that through the medium of English "the communication of useful knowledge will demolish the ancient learning and religion of Hindustan."[20]

This is in decided contrast to William Carey, who was a committed Orientalist throughout his career. This is significant not only because he remained a committed Orientalist even in the heyday of the Anglicist infusion in India, but because Carey's commitment to Orientalism preceded the later birth of British Orientalism, led by such well-known Orientalists as W. Jones, H. T. Colebrooke, and E. Burnouf, who began to write about the glory of the Hindu past and the erudition of the Sanskrit tradition, philosophy, and literature. Long before Orientalism was in vogue, Carey had diligently applied himself to the mastery of Indian languages such as Sanskrit, Bengali, Marathi, and Hindi. By the time of Carey's death in 1834, he had translated the entire Bible into six languages, the New Testament into 23 more, and various portions were available in about ten other languages. As an Orientalist, Carey is widely regarded even among Indian historians as the "father of Bengali prose."[21]

---

19. Alexander Duff, *The Church of Scotland's India Mission: or, A Brief Exposition of the Principles on which that Mission Has Been Conducted in Calcutta* (Edinburgh: John Waugh, 1835), 20. This is an archival pamphlet recording an address given by Duff at the General Assembly of the Church of Scotland on May 25, 1835.

20. Duff, *Church*, 10, 20.

21. Chand, *History*, 2:187. Carey is responsible for the first comprehensive grammar of Bengali and the preparation of an eighty thousand–word dictionary that set the standard for the emergence of Bengali prose.

Carey was a pioneer in translating Indian cultural and religious texts for popular Indian and English distribution. He translated portions of the Mahabharata and the Ramayana as early as 1802. In 1807, he joined the Bengal Asiatic Society, which he attended for twenty-six years, missing less than a dozen meetings during that entire period. He produced dictionaries and grammars of Bengali, Marathi, Telugu, Punjabi, and Sanskrit, all remarkable testimonies to the Orientalist commitment of William Carey.

The significance of the nineteenth-century debate between the Anglicist and Orientalist schools can hardly be overestimated in light of contemporary missiology. Twentieth-century missiology routinely emphasizes the importance of learning from the host culture and, as far as possible, indigenizing the gospel message into native soil, rather than extracting the people group out of their culture into a foreign system of thought and language. Indeed, the contextual translatability of the Christian gospel has become one of the hallmarks of both modern Protestant missions and the field of missiology. We remain indebted to William Carey, who understood this point long before the advent of missiology as a field of study.

CAREY'S DEFINITION AND FOCUS OF MISSIONS

Third, Carey understood that missions must be defined as and focused on those who have no current access to the gospel.

The modern connotations of the word "missions" are of relatively recent origin. Until the sixteenth century, the term was used in a Trinitarian context to refer to the sending of the Son by the Father and of the Holy Spirit by the Father and the Son. The Reformers never use the word "missions" in any of their writings to convey our understanding of the *apostolate* dimension of the church's life, propagating the faith globally. In fact, it was the Jesuits who were the first to use the term "mission" to refer to the spread of the Christian faith among people who did not belong to the Catholic Church.[22] Since the advent of the nineteenth-century modern missionary movement, the church's understanding of missions has gone through several critical phases of development, which exceed the limitations of this chapter to explore. However, from an evangelical point of view, at the heart of missions lies the vital distinction between those who have access to the gospel and those who do not. Missions is ultimately about spreading the gospel to those who have not yet heard or understood the gospel of Jesus Christ.

22. Bosch, *Transforming*, 1.

One of the pressing challenges to evangelicals today concerning missions is the failure to recognize this distinction. One of the most important legacies of the modern missiologists Donald McGavran (1897–1990) and Ralph Winter (1924–2009) has been their emphasis on unreached people groups who have no access to the gospel. Winter is known among missiologists around the globe for his impassioned address at the 1974 International Congress on World Evangelization in Lausanne, Switzerland, where he called for an emphasis on unreached peoples or ethnic groups who have no access to the gospel. He spoke of "hidden" peoples who cannot hear the gospel and therefore cannot respond because there are simply no Christians resident within the ethnic group. Donald McGavran, in his *Bridges to God* and *Ethnic Realities and the Church*,[23] has also helped to highlight the importance of the church prioritizing those with no access to the gospel and keeping missions focused on bringing the gospel to those who otherwise could not hear.[24]

Despite the efforts of contemporary missiologists such as Winter and McGavran, the North American church continues to blur the meaning of the word "missions" such that it encompasses anything the church does outside the four walls of its building. The problem with calling everything the church does by the term "missions" is that it dilutes the urgency of prioritizing the church's task toward those who currently have no access to the gospel. This problem is exacerbated when one looks at formerly "Christianized" lands and can find no real difference between nominal Christians and non-Christians. Therefore, it often seems like a false distinction to distinguish between "local evangelism" and "missions" or between "home missions" and "foreign missions." Now that the *corpus Christianum* has evaporated, some argue that even the home front is a mission field. Why send troops out to foreign lands when there is a raging battle at our own doorstep? From a missiological perspective, this line of reasoning has done much to dilute the issue of access that is so vital to a proper view of missions.

There can be little doubt that the growing secularism and violence in American culture should call us to redouble our efforts to communicate

23. Donald A. McCavran, *Bridges to God: A Study in the Strategy of Missions* (New York: Friendship, 1955) and *Ethnic Realities and the Church: Lessons from India* (South Pasadena, CA: William Carey Library, 1979).

24. Donald McGavran's homogenous unit principle is, in the context of this paper, used to highlight McGavran's commitment to missions as targeting "peoples," not merely "places." McGavran and Winter almost single-handedly changed the vocabulary of missions from discussing "unreached territories" (the language of the 1910 World Missionary Conference in Edinburgh) to "unreached peoples."

the gospel more effectively to our own culture. However, this should not distract us from the compelling truth that missions-minded Christians must continue to remind the church about the "access issue." There are still nearly three thousand people groups in India with little or no access to the gospel. Thousands of other ethnic groups have been identified around the world with either no Christians resident within the group or so few that there is no viable gospel witness.[25] This great burden must lie at the heart of our understanding of missions.

With this background, it is once more evident how insightful and relevant William Carey's writings are in this contemporary debate. Carey demonstrates a remarkable clarity regarding what the church should defend as true missions, despite many other important and vital ministries that Christians should necessarily be involved in as the people of God. In 1792, Carey wrote his famous pamphlet entitled *An Enquiry into the Obligations of Christians to Use Means for the Conversion of the Heathens*. This eighty-seven-page missiological pamphlet has been called the *magna carta* of the modern missionary movement. This document reveals insights into Carey's appreciation of anthropology, linguistics, strategic planning, and theological debate that continue to remain instructive in modern missiological discussions.[26]

To illustrate this point, we will examine Carey's emphasis on the issue of access long before it was articulated by modern missiologists. The document, commonly known simply as *An Enquiry*, is divided into several strategic sections. First, there is a *theological* section that seeks to address and respond to the theological position of writers such as Johann Gerhard and Philipp Nicolai, noted earlier. The second is a *historical* section that surveys the history of global missions up to that time. Carey is not only aware of the apostolic traditions, but he is inspired by figures much closer to his time, such as David Brainerd (1718–1747), who sought to bring the gospel to indigenous tribes of the middle American colonies. A third section deals with *practical and logistical* issues that were often cited as reasons for the church not sending out missionaries. It is in the first section dealing

---

25. The best source for identifying unreached people groups is Todd M. Johnson and Kenneth Ross, eds., *Atlas of Global Christianity* (Edinburgh: Edinburgh University Press, 2009).

26. More than one-fourth of the pamphlet deals with charts showing the geographic size and populations and religious adherence throughout the world. George Smith, in 1885, called it "the first and still the greatest missionary treatise in the English language."

with theological issues that Carey wrestles with the issue of access as central to a proper understanding of missions. He wrote as follows:

> It has been objected that there are multitudes in our own nation, and within our immediate spheres of action, who are as ignorant as the South-Sea savages, and that therefore we have work enough at home, without going into other countries. That there are thousands in our own land as far from God as possible, I readily grant, and that this ought to excite us to ten-fold diligence to our work, and in attempts to spread divine knowledge amongst them is a certain fact; but that it ought to supersede all attempts to spread the gospel in foreign parts seems to want proof. Our own countrymen have the means of grace, and may attend on the word preached if they choose it. They have the means of knowing the truth, and faithful ministers are placed in almost every part of the land, whose spheres of action might be much extended if their congregations were but more hearty and active in the cause; but with them the case is widely different, who have no Bible, no written language, no ministers.[27]

Carey's words, though written over two hundred years ago, clearly demonstrate his appreciation for the current missiological debate about the need for the church to give special priority to those who have no access to the gospel.

CONCLUSION

Although William Carey lived almost two centuries before the advent of missiology, his writings and missionary practice prove him to be an able missiologist. His missionary achievements are notable precisely because he was a missiological pioneer. There were many notable Protestant missionaries before Carey. They included the early pioneers of Protestant missions, Bartholomew Ziegenbalg and Heinrich Plutschau, the great missionaries in North America, John Eliot and David Brainerd, and, of course, the entire Moravian missionary movement from the estate of Nicholas von Zinzendorf. Carey is known as the father of the modern missionary movement because he created new paradigms for thought and new structures for action in the missiological endeavor. He demonstrated that he was not only a missionary practitioner, but a missiologist as well. Indeed, if it were not for the missiological perspective of William Carey, it is doubtful whether he would have been successful in mobilizing and helping to stimulate the largest wave of missionary expansion in history.

27. Carey, *Enquiry*, 13.

3

Shoemaker and Missionary, William Carey

A *Dalit* Christian Perspective

CHAKRAVARTHY R. ZADDA

AS EARLY AS THE 1800s, William Carey sowed the seeds of modernization in Bengal, which was at that time the political, intellectual, and cultural hub of India. In recognition of Carey's contributions to this great nation, in his 1874 book, *Sekal O Ekal*, Rajnarayan Basu includes Carey along with four other honored Englishmen as the architects of the Indian Renaissance.[1] Basu wrote in Sanskrit:

> *"Hare, Colvin, Palmerasheha, Carey, Marshmanastatha*
> *Pancha gorah smarennityammaha pataknashanam"*
> (Hare, Colvin, Palmer, Carey, and Marshman are five learned white men, who will be remembered always with reverence.)[2]

There has been a great deal of literature published since the nineteenth century about the life and work of William Carey from different perspectives. The objective here is to examine the life of Carey through *Dalit* lenses.

1. See Malay Dewanji, *William Carey and The Indian Renaissance* (Delhi: Indian Society for Promoting Christian Knowledge, 1996), 2.

2. Rajnarayan Basu, *Sekal O Ekal* (Calcutta, 1874). This is the author's translation.

This is for three specific reasons. First, the story is told to celebrate the legacy of Carey, which is an integral part of the *Dalit* Christian heritage. It was surprising to note that only less than twenty-five percent of *Dalit* Christians have heard about Carey and his legacy, and my hope is to remedy that. Second, the story is told to encourage a critical consciousness in *Dalits*, opening their eyes to their historical oppression and making them aware of the need for liberation. Third, my final reason for telling this story is to provide motivation and inspiration for the cause of *Dalit* emancipation.[3]

SETTING THE CONTEXT: WHO ARE DALITS?

Dalits are "outcastes" falling outside the traditional four-fold caste system consisting of Brahmin, Kshatriya, Vaishya, and Shudra classes. They are considered impure and polluting and are therefore physically and socially excluded and isolated from the rest of society. The word *Dalit* comes from the Sanskrit root *dal-* and means "broken, ground-down, downtrodden, or oppressed."[4] Those previously known as Untouchables, Depressed Classes, and Harijans are today increasingly adopting the term *Dalit* as a name for themselves. *Dalit* refers to one's caste rather than class; it applies to members of those menial castes, which have born the stigma of "untouchability" because of the extreme impurity and pollution connected with their traditional occupations.

WHAT IS THE PRESENT STATUS OF DALITS?

Dalits represent a community of 170 million in India, constituting seventeen percent of the population. One out of every six Indians is a *Dalit*, yet due to their caste identity, *Dalits* regularly face discrimination and violence, which prevent them from enjoying the basic human rights and dignity promised to all citizens of India. The atrocities committed against these vulnerable groups have been escalating each year. The statistics from the Indian National Crime Bureau reveal that in 2010, recorded crimes against *Dalits* totaled 32,712, while 67,571 were crimes against religious minorities

---

3. As a Baptist Christian and an ordained minister in the Samavesam of Telugu Baptist Churches denomination of India, I deem it a privilege to write a chapter in honor of William Carey.

4. James Massey, *Dalits in India* (New Delhi: Manohar, 1995), 15.

(Christians and Muslims during riots).[5] Thus *Dalits* and religious minorities, even after sixty-four years of independence, continue to suffer discrimination, exploitation, and atrocities at the hands of the upper castes.

Caste-based social systems extend beyond India, finding corollaries in Nepal, Pakistan, Sri Lanka, and Bangladesh, as well as other countries outside of South Asia. More than 260 million people worldwide suffer from this "hidden apartheid" of segregation, exclusion, and discrimination.

WHAT IS THE STATUS OF DALIT CHRISTIANS?

Of the twenty-four million Christians in India, *Dalits* constitute about nineteen million, mostly living in the southern states of Andhra Pradesh, Karnataka, Kerala and Tamil Nadu. It is important to note that ninety-five percent of Christians in Andhra Pradesh come from two outcaste communities, whose traditional caste professions were weaving and leather tanning. Thus the present-day church in Andhra Pradesh is typically a community of weavers and cobblers.

Dalit Christians are thrice discriminated: within the church, in society, and by the state. *Dalits* embraced Christianity, seeking a better life with dignity. But they experience discrimination even within the church. The dominant caste converts do not accept the people of lower castes as their equals. Unchristian and discriminatory practices are being continued within the church. Second, whether Christians or Hindus, the dominant caste people treat the *Dalit* Christians with the same contempt and subject them to the same ill-treatment as their Hindu counterparts. Finally, the state itself discriminates against the Christian *Dalits* on the basis of religion, denying their privileges granted through the Presidential Order.[6] Instead of caste and socio-economic backwardness being the criteria for

5. Indian National Crime Records Bureau, "Crime in India 2010," Figures at a Glance 2010 (New Delhi: National Crime Records Bureau, 2011), iii, online: http://ncrb.nic.in/CII2010/Compendium2010.pdf.

6. The third paragraph of the Constitution (Scheduled Castes) Order, 1950, popularly known as the Presidential Order, stipulates that "no person who professes a religion different from the Hindu religion shall be deemed to be a member of a Scheduled Caste." By restricting the benefits to a particular religion, the order has divided the entire *Dalit* community on the basis of religion. Ministry of Social Justice and Empowerment: Government of India, *The Constitution (Scheduled Caste) [(Union Territories)] Order 1951* Co.32, online: http://socialjustice.nic.in/scorder1951.php#f2.

reservation, the linkage of caste with the religion (Christianity) is treated as the crux of the problem.

CAREY'S SIMILARITIES WITH THE DALITS

William Carey had many similar experiences to those of present day *Dalits*. It was in a small thatched cottage in the village of Paulerspury, near Towcester, in the county of Northamptonshire in England that William Carey was born on August 17, 1761. To a very large extent the England of those days, like India today, was a land of villages. Paulerspury is said to have had a population of about eight hundred.[7] Carey's parents, Edmund Carey and Elizabeth Wills, were weavers, and from early morning until nightfall, their little house reverberated with the dull thud of the loom on which they earned their living. Edmund's mother, who lost her husband when Edmund was seven, continued to live with him until her death. Like most of the *Dalit* couples today who earn less than $5 a day, Edmund and Elizabeth together could not have earned twenty shillings a week, and possibly considerably less—perhaps only half that sum.[8] With two small children and an aged mother they had great difficulty in making ends meet.

When Carey turned six, his father Edmund was appointed the master for the village school. With this new job came new possibilities. The family moved into the schoolhouse at the other end of the village. Carey spent eight important years of his childhood in this house.[9] The village surroundings and the country scenery nurtured Carey's life, and did much to make him the agriculturist and naturalist of Bengal.

The schoolhouse had a garden where Carey not only played but spent time with the plants. Carey received his first gardening lessons from his uncle Peter, who was a gardener in the same village. Carey worked on his father's garden until it was the best kept in the whole neighborhood. This passion for gardening continued, and later in his life he created the botanical park at Serampore, which for more than half a century was unique in Southern Asia.

---

7. Frank Deaville Walker, *William Carey: Missionary Pioneer and Statesman* (London: Student Christian Movement, 1926), 12.

8. Walker, *William Carey*, 15.

9. George Smith, *The Life of William Carey, D.D.: Shoemaker and Missionary* (London: R & R Clark, 1885), 4.

About his childhood education, Carey wrote, "My education was that which is generally esteemed good in country villages."[10] Though the country school lessons were limited in scope, Carey's desire for knowledge pushed his boundaries of learning. Carey's sister recollected her mother's remarks: "She has heard him in the night, when the family were asleep, casting accompts [old system of arithmetic]."[11] He was from childhood intent in the pursuit of knowledge. Whatever he began, he finished; difficulties never seemed to discourage his mind.[12]

Deaville Walker, in his book *William Carey: Missionary Pioneer and Statesman*, noted the words of Carey, "From my infancy I was accustomed to read the scriptures."[13] Being the son of the schoolmaster, Carey had an educational advantage on which he capitalized. As he grew up, this thirst for knowledge increased. In addition to mathematics, he began to learn Latin. At the age of twelve, he memorized sixty pages of Dyche's *Latin Vocabulary*.[14] He was also fond of drawing and painting, in which he made considerable progress.

He read most of the books available for him in the village and had a special taste for some. Carey wrote, "I chose to read books of science, history, voyages etc. Novels and Plays always disgusted me, and I avoided them."[15] His frequent conversations about the adventures of Columbus with his friends earned him the same nickname.

The passions that were planted into the young life of Carey bore greater fruit later in the different fields of education, language, literature, science, and social reform. Of all the things that Carey learned, the most important was his great belief in the importance of education for social transformation and liberation.

Though Carey was an enthusiastic student, the family's poverty could not get him beyond the free village school. At the age of fourteen, he began to work as an agricultural laborer. Because of a skin disease, William could not work in the sun, so Edmund apprenticed his son to Clarke Nichols, a shoemaker.

10. Dewanji, *William Carey*, 3.

11. Smith, *Life*, 5.

12. Walker, *William Carey*, 18.

13. Walker, *William Carey*, 16.

14. Walker, *William Carey*, 24.

15. Smith, *Life*, 7.

As an apprentice, Carey would learn to prepare the leather, to use the tools of his craft, and to cut the welts and uppers, the soles and heels. Also once a week he walked the five miles to Northampton with a load of boots for some dealers.

Unfortunately, the shoemaking profession did not work well with Carey. In 1779 Nichols died before Carey could finish his term, so he had to join with Thomas Old of Hackleton for a low wage. While he was working for Old, Carey married Dorothy Plackett, Old's sister-in-law. Dorothy came from a very pious family but was not educated. She was unable to sign her name, and the marriage register contains a very badly formed cross.[16] Carey and Dorothy loved each other dearly.

After two and a half years, Old died, leaving the business to Carey. Unfortunately, Carey had to close down the business after a brief time, and in 1785 he moved to Moulton, where he began to teach in a primary school in addition to making shoes. Here three of his sons, Felix, William, and Peter, were born. During this time he became connected to the church and before long, he was called to be the pastor for a small church in Harvey Lane, closer to Leicester city. Carey spent twelve years of his life as a cobbler, from sixteen to twenty-eight, until he went to Leicester.[17]

It is typical of *Dalit* Christians to presuppose that missionaries belonging to economically high-class society had high social status in the countries of their origin. Whether or not this is true, they are put on a high pedestal and given great respect. The opposite of this stereotypical thinking is to assume that the missionaries have no idea or experience of what it means to be an outcaste or low class. Carey's earlier life in England breaks this stereotype and invites the *Dalits* to see him as one among them, if not completely but at least in a limited way. His experience belonging to a cobbler family, dealing with economic constraints, having limited educational opportunities and an uncertain future, being an apprentice, earning low wages, and generally belonging to a group of marginalized and poor people, can well resonate with the socioeconomic situation of the present day *Dalits*.

CAREY'S ENCOUNTER WITH THE DALITS

William Carey, along with John Thomas, landed in Calcutta on November 11, 1793. At this very same time, Wilberforce was unsuccessful in his

16. Walker, *William Carey*, 43.

17. Smith, *Life*, 10.

attempts to legalize the travel of schoolmasters and other approved persons with the East India Company for the purpose of the religious and moral improvement of the Indians. The effects of this were felt even before Carey and John Thomas left for India. Carey was denied a license by the East India Company to go to India. Though it was a criminal offense to get into India without a license, both missionaries managed to enter the country through the help of the Danish government.

The first seven years in India prepared Carey for the real ministry, of which he had dreamt for years. The fear of the East India Company and financial challenges had pushed Carey to move from place to place. After living in Calcutta for a month, Carey found it was expensive to live there so he moved with his family to Bandel, which was then a Portuguese colony. Faced with the Catholic presence in Bandel he moved to Nabadwip but could not find stability there, so within a month he was back to Calcutta. With the help of his *munshi* (clerk/secretary) Ram Basu, Carey found temporary shelter near Manicktla. On February 6, 1794, Ram Basu procured Carey a piece of land rent free in Debhatta village, in the midst of the thick forest of the Sunderbans.

Carey saw the missions principles that he had outlined in his famous tract, *An Enquiry*, coming alive. First, a missionary must be one of the companions and equals of the people to whom he is sent; and second, the mission must, as soon as possible, become indigenous, self-supporting, and self-propagating.[18] Carey decided to move immediately to Debhatta so that he could farm the land and support his mission.

Debhatta, being an isolated place in the deep jungles, introduced the Careys to "real" Indian life, which was quite different from what they experienced around Calcutta. It was three days' journey on the boat by narrow saltwater rivers into the forest, which was almost entirely uninhabited, but for the wild beasts and reptiles. Carey, recounting this journey said, "But no one dares go on shore, so as to venture a hundred yards from the boat.... The nights were loud with croaking of the frogs, the chorus of innumerable crickets, the cry of the Jackal, the laughter of the Hyena and the roar of the tigers."[19] The journey itself was a terrifying experience for the Careys.

Traveling through the small villages exposed Carey to the deep socio-religious enslavement of the natives, including his brief stop at a village to see the ritual performed for the goddess of power, *Kali*.

18. Smith, *Life*, 80.
19. As quoted in Walker, *William Carey*, 158.

Being in the midst of the jungle, Debhatta was likely inhabited by mostly outcaste and tribal communities. It is seldom that the caste communities choose to live in such remote and dangerous places. Poverty and social backwardness of these communities had deprived them of the basic necessities, but oppressive religious structures were strongly ruling over them. Upon their arrival, the Careys were told of recent incidents of people being attacked by the tigers, which forced them to leave the place. However, Carey's possession of a gun was an encouragement for these people to return. It was here in Debhatta that Carey may have had his first interaction with *Dalits*.

A. H. Oussoren remarks, "On the river Jubona lay many villages and the people were full of interest for this stranger and his Gospel."[20] Though it may have been possible that he met some outcastes during his time at Calcutta and other places, his close association with the Brahmin community could have prevented any personal interaction with *Dalits*.

Carey stayed in Debhatta for four months before he moved to Modhnoboti to take a job as manager for an indigo factory. The factory Carey had to manage was at Modhnoboti, thirty-two miles north of Malda. Carey's acceptance called for a long journey of three hundred miles across rivers through the jungle. For the next six years, Carey worked there in Modhnoboti.[21]

Geographically, Modhnoboti was extremely different from Debhatta. It was open country, with rice fields stretching as far as the eye could see, and with mango and banyan trees. Carey remarked, "There was little need to fear wild beasts, for although there were a few wild buffaloes, hogs, crocodiles and even tigers in the neighborhood, they seldom attacked human beings."[22] But Carey could not anticipate that humans can perpetuate greater fears than the wild. The fertility of the soil and favorable living conditions made Modhnoboti a typical Indian village, inhabited by both the caste people living in the center and outcaste people living outside the village. There was a strong religious hold on the people through socio-economic disparities and boundaries of caste.

Carey's workmen insisted that he make an offering to the goddess Kali for prosperous indigo making at the beginning of the season. It came to him as a surprise, probably even a shock, when he heard the next day that

20. Aalbertinus H. Oussoren, *William Carey, Especially His Missionary Principles* (Leiden: Sijthoff's Uitgeversmaatschappij, 1945), 61.

21. Ibid., 62.

22. Walker, *William Carey*, 158.

they actually offered a child from the outcaste community as a sacrifice to the goddess.[23] The news that the prosperity of his business was at the cost of an innocent life broke Carey's heart, but the real tragedy had yet to come.

The differences among the people were so glaring that the outcastes had a different dialect. Regarding his conversations with the outcaste communities, Carey wrote, "At first I had some difficulty with the language; for though by this time I was able to speak a little Bengali, but found that the workpeople spoke a dialect which differs from true Bengali, so I have to work hard to understand them and to make them understand me."[24]

Life in Modhnoboti had a very drastic influence on the life of Carey and provided for him a groundbreaking examination of Indian social life. Until that point, Carey had been objectively studying, learning, and understanding the socio-religious life of the natives as an outsider. The close association with the Brahmin community and hiring Ram Bose as his *munshi* gave Carey some upper-caste privileges in the society, which many times Carey might have taken for granted, or not even noticed. The rent-free land offered to Carey at Debhatta is one good example. The local *Zamindar* would only have offered it rent free for a white man, an unimaginable scenario for an outcaste.

Carey realized the real challenges of social discrimination for outsiders during his most depressed time. While Carey himself was suffering with severe fever and dysentery, his third son Peter, who was five, was likewise seized with dysentery following an attack of fever. Tragically, the child passed away within a few hours. Carey could not find anyone to help him with the funeral. The religious rites of purity and impurity so rigidly bound the social system that no one could be of any help. Though there were two carpenters at the factory, Carey could not induce either of them to make a coffin. In the hope of getting some help for the funeral preparations, Carey sent people seven or eight miles away, but to no avail. After a long negotiation, four Muslims, risking their identity, agreed to dig the grave. Out of two to three hundred laborers then employed on the estate, not even one would risk breaking caste by carrying the little boy to the grave. Having no other way, Carey and Dorothy decided that they would take him to the burial place. Finally, in the last moment, a man of sweeper caste and a boy who had lost caste were prevailed upon to perform the duty and to secure the little grave against the attacks of jackals.

23. Walker, *William Carey*, 171.
24. Walker, *William Carey*, 170.

The story did not end there; the local community excommunicated the four Muslims. Carey sent two men to bring the Muslim leader to his house by force and kept him under virtual house arrest while a judge was fetched to settle the matter. He was finally made to eat with the excommunicates so the four could be restored in the community.[25]

Local religious customs pushed the Careys to the limits of their tolerance. Dorothy might have been able to take the loss of her son, but the agony of feeling victimized by the Indian social customs caused this countrywoman to fall into melancholia, which later developed into insanity. William, on the other hand, wanted to fight against this system of human discrimination. It was through this experience that William realized what it meant to be an outcaste, and how this discrimination engulfed the lives of millions of outcastes in India. William Carey charged himself to use all the means available in his vicinity and ability to abolish inhuman practices perpetuated in the name of religion. He committed himself to learning the Hindu scriptures to not only identify their religious sanctions but also to counter them using their own scriptures. It was this new commitment that informed the holistic approach of the Serampore mission.

A suffering God in Christ became the source of Carey's missions theology. While it had evolved from the context of physical suffering and *dukha* ("sorrow"), it was nevertheless rooted in the depth of God's pain for the liberation of the "unsaved" and the rejected. Carey learned the meaning of the suffering God from the shackles of the ongoing struggles of the poor, living hand-to-mouth; from ill-treatment, suppression, and captivity; and from an unfailing, continuous, and constant reflection and dialogue with the Holy Bible.

CAREY'S CONTRIBUTION TO THE DALITS

George Udney, a civil servant who owned an indigo factory, suffered several financial losses, forcing Carey to move from Modhnoboti to Khidurpur, where he bought an indigo factory with the help of Udney and the money he had saved. But the Khidurpur factory was no success at all.[26] The place was obscure and unhealthy, and the successor of Udney at Malda was very hostile. Meanwhile, the arrival of more missionary friends to Serampore

---

25. Vishal Mangalwadi and Ruth Mangalwadi, *William Carey and the Regeneration of India* (Mussoorie, U.P., India: Nivedit Good Books, 1997), 38.

26. Walker, *William Carey*, 68.

motivated Carey to move to Serampore to join them on January 1, 1800.[27] The following are seven ways that Carey contributed to the *Dalits*: 1) translation, 2) caste system, 3) school and boarding home, 4) school for the girls, 5) higher and theological education, 6) agricultural and botanical gardens, and 7) prohibition acts.

Of all of Carey's contributions—particularly his contributions to the *Dalit* community—translating the Bible was his greatest. Carey wrote, "When I first entered on the translation of the scriptures in the Bengali language, I thought that if ever I should live to see it completed I should say with Simeon, 'Lord now lettest thou thy servant depart in peace.'"[28] By the end of his life, Carey had translated the whole Bible into six major Indian languages and portions of it into twenty-nine other languages, making a total of thirty-five.

In the years subsequent to Carey's mission, conversions were often initiated by local leaders who now had access to either a part or the whole of the Bible in their own language. Having the Bible available in the vernacular also aided the subsequent missionaries in the process of evangelization of the *Dalit* communities. Today seventy percent of the Christians in India are *Dalits*. In their struggles to emancipate themselves from the oppressive caste system, *Dalits* choose conversion as a means of protest and as a source of liberation.

Carey not only rejected the caste system, but practically set aside caste distinctions among the converts. He did not see the reflection of God's kingdom if the practice of caste distinction was still retained in the Christian church. He advocated for inter-caste marriages and also invited them as equals at the Lord's table. Krishna Pal, who was from the low-caste, was ordained and appointed to work among the Khasis at Pandua. Unfortunately, *Dalit* Christians still struggle from discrimination they face within the church. Nearly two hundred years after Carey's mission, the church in India has come out boldly against caste distinctions. The National Council of Churches in India has given a call for zero tolerance for caste discrimination in the church.[29]

27. His colleagues included William Ward, the Marshmans, the Brunsdons, the Grants, and Mary Tidd Fountain.

28. Robert Young, *Modern Missions: Their Trials and Triumphs* (New York: Cassell, 1884), 22.

29. "Indian Churches: 'Zero Tolerance' for Caste Discrimination," News & Resources, International Dalit Solidarity Network, November 1, 2010, online: http://idsn.org/news-resources/idsn-news/read/archive/2010/november/article/indian-churches-zero-tolerance-for-caste-discrimination/128/.

Carey had great hope that education would lead to the social regeneration of societies. When he was in Malda during 1794 he started a school. But after a few months, the parents took their children away, since the children needed to work to help earn money for their poor families. To sustain the school, Carey had to provide food and clothing to the children at his own expense.

When the Serampore mission wanted to start a school for the children as an income to the mission under the leadership of the Marshmans, Carey suggested the need for boarding schools, based on his experience in Malda. The regular schools served only Europeans and the caste-conscious communities who preferred not to live or eat with others. The concept of education through boarding school was primarily oriented to the outcaste communities. The poor parents who could not afford to feed their children brought them to the boarding school. Ruth Mangalwadi observed, "Free schools for the low castes and the outcastes were always a chief feature of Carey's work, and these were started within a twenty-mile radius of Serampore where almost 8,000 children attended."[30] It was this system of schools with boarding facilities attached that most helped the *Dalits* to receive education.

The missionaries from the other societies later on adopted this as they ministered the gospel to the outcaste communities. Ninety-five percent of the *Dalit* communities across the nation today receive their education from these missions boarding schools.

Education of females was another gift offered by the Serampore mission to the *Dalit* communities. Carey, with the help of Hannah Marshman, took the lead in beginning the revolution of modern education for the women of rural Bengal, which led in turn to the founding of other girls' schools in Benares, Dhaka, and Allahabad. The immediate impact of these schools was apparent to all observers. Ann Judson observed in a letter to her sister about the Mission Charity School near Carey's house that it had "two-hundred boys and nearly as many girls – chiefly children picked up from the streets, of no caste."[31] Ann Judson's remarks clearly highlight the commitment of the Serampore mission to the outcaste communities, particularly to the girls.

---

30. Vishal Mangalwadi and Ruth Mangalwadi, *The Legacy of William Carey: A Model for the Transformation of a Culture* (Wheaton, IL: Crossway, 1999), 40.

31. Mangalwadi and Mangalwadi, *Legacy*, 40.

During his youth, Carey learned the importance of higher education for social transformation and liberation. Carey was instrumental in launching the Serampore College in order to offer higher education in the vernacular. The goal envisaged by Carey in the foundation of the Serampore College was something unique. The College was for the instruction of Indian Christians and other youth in Eastern Literature and European Sciences. The College was conceived of as "the apex of an educational system where Indian youth could be educated in a setting where the classical Hindu, Islamic and Christian as well as scientific and secular cultures can dialogue with each other producing an indigenous synthetic humanist culture."[32] To crown it all, a theological institute was founded as a part of the Arts and Science College to prepare the future leaders of the church to be in dialogue with the Indian and European Sciences to benefit church and society. Even today, Serampore College is the only institution of higher learning in India to confer recognized degrees in the field of Theological Education.[33]

As Carey traveled from one plantation to another in the surrounding villages, overseeing the growth of the indigo crops, he developed an interest in India's flora and fauna, and he converted part of his indigo estate into a garden where he raised flowering and fruit trees. It appears that from this Modhnoboti plantation, Carey started regular correspondence with Dr. William Roxburgh at the Sibpore Botanic Garden, sending fruits and pressed plants for identification. It is easy to understand how he earned the nickname "Plantation Padre."[34] Carey also began to understand, through the process of developing the indigo crops, how much India's populace depended on agriculture for its livelihood. He diagnosed the reason for India's perpetual rural poverty and suggested the solution might lie in the improvement of farm technology. He took practical interest in it and wrote letters to England requesting scythes, sickles, plough wheels, and other small agricultural implements, confirming his commitment to and genuine love for poor agricultural laborers and farmers.

The patriarchal society of India, with religious sanctions, was oppressing the females through polygamy, female infanticide, child marriage, widow

32. M. M. Thomas, "Bicentenary Inaugural Address: 11th November 1992," *Indian Journal of Theology* 35, no. 1 (1993) 6–7, online: http://www.biblicalstudies.org.uk/pdf/ijt/35-1_002.pdf.

33. The author of this chapter is a grateful alumnus of the Senate of Serampore College.

34. S. Pearce Carey, *William Carey, D.D., Fellow of Linnaean Society* (London: Hodder and Stoughton, 1925), 14.

burning, temple prostitution, and female illiteracy. The Hindu lawgiver Manu had put women in a worse place than animals, for they were divinely predestined to play an inferior role. Carey was the first man to stand against both the ruthless murders and the widespread oppression of women.[35] He began to conduct systematic sociological and scriptural research. He published reports both in Bengal and in England to raise public opinion and to protest. He influenced a generation of Indian youth from Fort William College to resist these evils. It was Carey's persistent battle against *Sati* for nearly twenty-five years that finally led to Lord Bentinck's edict, in 1829, banning one of the most heinous religious practices in the world: widow burning.

Widow burning was not a practice of the *Dalits*, since they do not burn the dead. However, it was forced upon the *Dalit* women by the religion to be buried alive. Carey described how a pit was dug and the widow sat in it with the body of her dead husband in her lap. The family then threw in mud until the earth reached the head of the suffocating widow.

The anti-widow-burning movement did not ignore other heinous practices such as leper burning. The issue of the inhuman treatment and lack of social acceptance of lepers caused Carey further grief. The ghastly sight that he encountered of a leper being burned alive by his own mother and sister, so that he could be purified in the next birth, moved Carey once again to action. The result was that "one of India's oldest leprosy hospitals came into being."[36]

Infanticide was another atrocious religious custom practiced in several forms. One form was to seek prosperity. Carey remembered his workmen offering an infant as a sacrifice to the goddess Kali in order to seek prosperity in business. A second form was to fulfill vows. Parents offered their children to the river goddess Ganges because of a vow they had made. It was considered a positive sign that the goddess had accepted the offering if crocodiles hungrily devoured the infant. A third form was to drive away the evil spirits. If an infant was sick, it was supposed that the baby was under the influence of an evil spirit. In this case the baby was put into a basket and hung up to a tree for three days. Only if the child survived was it considered that he or she was not under the influence of the evil spirit.

These superstitions particularly victimized the *Dalit* children. It was not necessarily that *Dalits* were practicing these rituals, but the caste communities were using the *Dalit* infants for their sacrifices. As Carey's

---

35. Mary Drewery, *William Carey: A Biography* (Grand Rapids: Zondervan. 1981), 80.

36. Oussoren, *William Carey*, 196.

concern for these victims of superstition became known, he was asked by the governor general to inquire into the numbers, nature, and reasons for this practice of infanticide. His report resulted in the practice being made illegal.

CONCLUSION

Carey's positive attitude toward Indian cultures, his desire for an indigenous theology, and his concern for the liberation of the downtrodden and for the creation of a healthy ecology and environment demonstrate the Christ-centered nature of his mission. He had a vision for an emerging India, based on the gospel values of truth, equality, liberty, and social justice.

Truly the role of William Carey in the making of modern India is significant. Because of divine grace and Carey's comprehensive knowledge, he succeeded in shaping Indian life in almost every area. Stephen Neill writes, "What David Livingston meant to Africa, William Carey meant to India and more."[37]

Carey was not a mere child of his time, but a pathfinder. He laid a foundation in virtually every area of the *Dalits'* emancipation and empowerment. His works were open to the lower castes and the outcastes, to women as well as men. This was true of the gospel, the churches, the schools, and the college. It applied to the basic rights for life and well-being, even for widows, lepers, and children.

His outstanding gifts of patience, persistence, determination, humility, and faithfulness are qualities that young *Dalit* Christians can draw upon as they continue to toil for their liberation. The selfless service offered by Carey for the liberation and emancipation of *Dalits* and marginalized communities in India has certainly earned him a place along with the great *Dalits,* Bhimrao Ramji Ambedkar and Mahatma Jotiba Govindrao Phule. William Carey's life and his legacy will be eternal in the history of the *Dalits.*

---

37. Stephen Neill, *A History of Christianity in India, 1707–1858* (Cambridge: University of Cambridge, 1985), 449.

4

Prophetic Precepts or Divine Preeminence?

Rammohan Roy vs. Joshua Marshman on the Significance of Jesus

Sean Doyle

In 1820, the Bengali intellectual Rammohan Roy published *The Precepts of Jesus: The Guide to Peace and Happiness*. Roy had already gained notoriety as an influential voice in what would later be designated "renascent Hinduism"; he vigorously denounced the veneration of Hindu images, polytheism, and widow burning (*sati*), promoting instead ethical monotheism and social concern in India. He found himself increasingly enamored with the moral values of Jesus of Nazareth; indeed, Roy asserted that the principles of Christ were convincing, transformative, and greatly profitable for humanity. The clarity of these pristine ethical values stood in stark contrast with the confusing, abstruse doctrines of institutional Christianity, as he deemed them. Roy also asserted that the miracle stories in the gospels would carry little weight with the peoples of India, since such fantastic tales abound in Hindu myths. And the historicity of the narrative portions of the gospels would likely be called into question by the intelligentsia. Therefore, in order to avoid unnecessary controversy and to persuade his fellow

Hindus of the sublime nature of the teachings of Jesus, Roy decided to publish a selection of the exalted precepts found in the Christian gospels.

The response from the missionary circles in Bengal came from Joshua Marshman, who worked closely with William Carey in Serampore.[1] Marshman was the editor of the Baptist periodical *Friend of India;* his published critiques of Roy's assertions were largely representative of the shared views of the members of the evangelical Serampore Trio. He expressed both admiration for the dissemination of the gospel principles and concern that the artificial separation of doctrine and ethics would injure the cause of truth in India. To promote Jesus as an inspired teacher would place him on the same level as Confucius and Mohammed, who, while significant voices for their own cultures and turbulent times, were less than divine. Marshman asserted that mere obedience to the moral sayings of Jesus would not be sufficient for an individual's salvation, especially if one denied the central dogmas of Christ's divinity and redemptive suffering. Roy responded in his *Appeal to the Christian Public* that the essential teachings of the gospels were faith and obedience to God, coupled with repentance and forgiveness. In Luke 10, when the expert in the law approached Jesus and inquired as to the means of eternal life, he was instructed by Christ to keep the commandments, thereby confirming the centrality of ethical conduct in the gospels. Marshman countered in the next edition of the *Friend of India* that there were two leading doctrines in the New Testament omitted by Roy's *Precepts*: "that God views all sin as so abominable, that the death of Jesus Christ alone can expiate its guilt; and that the human heart is so corrupt, that it must be renewed by the Divine Spirit before a man can enter heaven." These were the central teachings of the divine Savior Jesus, and "without these two dogmas, what is the Gospel?"[2]

Thus was initiated a series of published interchanges between Joshua Marshman and Rammohan Roy in which they debated with increasing intensity the identity and theological significance of Jesus. Roy was perhaps

---

1. Marshman (1768–1837) joined Carey in Bengal in 1799. He opened schools for English and Indian children and wrote a book of religious instruction for them. He also embarked upon major translation projects, such as the first rendering of the Bible into Chinese, as well as translations of Confucius's teachings and of the Hindu *Ramayana* epic. In 1818, Marshman started a Bengali newspaper and the monthly periodical *Friend of India*.

2. Marshman, "Remarks on Certain Observations in 'An Appeal to the Christian Public, in Defence of the Precepts of Jesus: By a Friend to Truth,'" in *A Defence of the Deity and Atonement of Jesus Christ: In Reply to Ram-mohun Roy of Calcutta* (London: Kingsbury, Parbury, and Allen, 1822), 10.

the most formidable advocate of the view that Jesus was to be greatly admired and embraced as a man whose ethical teachings could reform India, but that institutional Christianity's dogmas, such as the Trinity and the atonement, were unnecessary accretions that could be dismissed by those in progressive Hindu circles. In response, Marshman, articulating the theology of the Serampore Trio, advanced seven different arguments from the Scriptures meant to convince Roy and the reading public in India that Jesus was indeed divine; Roy in turn critiqued all seven arguments using the same gospel texts. The debate is historically important, for it illustrates the differing hermeneutical lenses of two of the most significant religious voices in nineteenth-century Bengal: those of the British Evangelical missionaries and of the early Hindu reform movement. Also, in terms of the history of world Christianity, Roy's arguments are a fascinating example of a non-Christian thinker engaging in high-level theological discussion, all the while using Christian sacred texts as sources of authority. Through close study of the debate and the published interchanges, it will be shown that despite Marshman's best efforts to persuade the Bengali intellectual of the divinity of Jesus through his seven arguments, Roy continually and insistently interprets Jesus as a *human* prophetic and messianic figure commissioned by God to reveal truth and perform signs. In his view, Jesus is not divine and is radically dependent upon God the Father for all his power and insight. This debate clearly demonstrates the intellectual resistance of progressive Hindus in the nineteenth century against orthodox Christian doctrines related to Jesus' unique status as a divine member of the Trinity.

ROY'S POLEMICS AND APOLOGETICS

Rammohan Roy was born in a village in the Hooghly district of West Bengal in 1772 to a Brahmin family that prospered in business exchanges with the local Muslim community. His childhood exposure to Islam prompted him to learn Persian and Arabic, and his early writings on universal monotheism likely reflect an appreciation of Akbar's search in the earlier Mogul era for the one true God who is revealed in all the great religions. Roy subsequently learned English and began to work in 1803 for the British East India Company, interacting for over a decade with the civilian officers of the Company, as well as William Carey, who was teaching at Fort William College in Calcutta.

In 1815, Roy started to compose treatises in which he argued that the texts of the Vedas and the early Vedantic theological tradition portrayed the purest version of Hinduism, expounding devotion to one supreme God. He regarded the contemporary expressions of Hindu spirituality as steeped in sacerdotalism, idolatry, and superstition; these modern variants are actually debased departures from pristine ancient monotheistic Hinduism. Roy appealed to pragmatic reason and common sense in both his admonition to return to "original" Hindu spirituality and in his pleas to reform certain social practices, such as *sati* and caste, for the greater common good. His skillful rhetoric in these polemic battles earned him admiration and fame, but also, from some quarters, censure as someone making unwarranted innovations in the tradition.

Roy founded his famous reform movement, the Brahmo Samaj, in 1828. This group galvanized the Bengali intelligentsia to assert confidently their identity as Hindus in a modernizing world over against traditionalists and triumphalist Westerners. Many similar movements were formed shortly afterward, both in agreement with Roy's overall vision and in fierce opposition to it. He traveled abroad to England, where he was warmly received by the Unitarian community. He died in Bristol in 1833.

In his quest to promote original, universal monotheism and pragmatic ethics, Roy found inspiration in the figure of Jesus and in the New Testament gospels, though he vocally rejected institutional Christianity. Missionaries who at first thought that Roy might be used by God to draw his peoples closer to Christ started to view Roy with suspicion and consternation, especially as his pamphlets began to sound more rationalistic and deistic in tone. His *Precepts of Jesus* and *Appeals* confirmed the worst fears of the missionaries: Roy denied the divinity of Jesus, utilizing his gifting for argumentative persuasion to challenge the orthodox reading of the gospel narratives. Joshua Marshman decided to engage Roy in public disputation by marshaling the following seven arguments in defense of Christ's divinity, thereby inviting a meticulous response from Roy.

MARSHMAN'S FIRST ARGUMENT:
NO ONE POSSESSES UBIQUITY BUT GOD HIMSELF[3]

Marshman begins his series of arguments by asserting that no mere creature is granted the capacity to be in two places at the same moment. Curiously,

3. The arguments are contained in Marshman, "Remarks," 23–24; Roy, "Second

in John 3:13, Jesus tells Nicodemus that he who "came down from heaven" is the Son of Man who is "in heaven"; Marshman interprets this seemingly contradictory declaration as a clear indication of Christ's divine omnipresence.[4] He buttresses his argument with Matthew 18:20, where Jesus delivers a present promise extending into the future that he will be in the midst of two or three who are gathered in his name. Both proof texts seem to convey a sense of Jesus' ubiquity spatially and temporally.

Roy, in his *Second Appeal*, challenges Marshman's reading of John 3:13 by emphasizing that the argument for omnipresence rests upon the assumption that the present tense of the Greek verb is best rendered with the English phrase "who is in heaven." Roy prefers to translate the phrase "who *was* in heaven," effectively undercutting Marshman's claim of Christ being in two places at one time. Roy provides several examples from John's gospel where the present tense of the Greek verb actually conveys a past or a future sense (11:8, 11:38, 13:6, 16:32). For example, Roy states that it is more logical to translate the Greek verb in John 8:58 (usually rendered "before Abraham was, I am") with the English past tense. Thus, *before* Abraham was, "I was." In addition, within quotations from prophetic writings, it is common for Greek verbs in the past tense actually to indicate occurrences that will take place in the future: "In Rama was there heard a voice" (Matt 2:18). Therefore, context and logic must determine the correct rendering of the tenses of these Greek verbs into English; according to Roy, Marshman has paid insufficient attention to such matters when quoting his proof texts. Roy also seeks to prove "the absence of Jesus from heaven during his stay on earth"[5] by citing texts such as John 6:62, where the Son of Man ascends

---

Appeal to the Christian Public, in Defence of the 'Precepts of Jesus,'" in *The Precepts of Jesus: The Guide to Peace and Happiness, Extracted from the Books of the New Testament Ascribed to the Four Evangelists. To Which Are Added, the First and Second Appeal to the Christian Public: In Reply to the Observations of Dr. Marshman, of Serampore* (New York: B. Bates, 1825), 175–79; Marshman, "Reply to 'A Second Appeal to the Christian Public, in Defence of the Precepts of Jesus,'" in *A Defence of the Deity and Atonement of Jesus Christ: In Reply to Ram-mohun Roy of Calcutta* (London: Kingsbury, Parbury, and Allen, 1822), 217–27; and Roy, "Final Appeal to the Christian Public, in Defence of the 'Precepts of Jesus,'" in *The Precepts of Jesus: The Guide to Peace and Happiness, Extracted from the Books of the New Testament Ascribed to the Four Evangelists. To Which Are Added, the First, Second, and Final Appeal to the Christian Public: In Reply to the Observations of Dr. Marshman of Serampore* (London: Unitarian Society, 1824), 611–26.

4. All biblical citations are from the King James Version, from which both Marshman and Roy quoted.

5. Roy, "Second Appeal," 177.

"up where he was before." He chides the logicality of ascribing the divine attribute of omnipresence to Jesus when the very human language of ascent and descent is often used for the Son of Man. As for Marshman's proof text of Jesus being gathered in the midst of two or three, Roy interprets the passage as indicating "his guidance to them when joined in searching for the truth, without preferring any claim to ubiquity."[6] A similar statement is found in Luke 16:29: "they have Moses and the Prophets; let them hear them." Obviously, the Jews "have" Moses in a figurative sense, rather than a literal one of omnipresence; the Christians "have" Jesus in a similar sense of the guidance of his teaching.

Marshman responds, "Is it not singular, and does it not seem almost ominous to our author's cause, that he cannot raise an objection to the ubiquity of Christ without adducing a new proof of his Godhead."[7] While it is true that sometimes in poetry, prophecy, or lively narration the present Greek tense is used to convey events in the past, John 8:58 is an example of didactic instruction where Christ refers to himself as the Eternal I AM; this bold declaration was correctly interpreted by the religious leaders as a claim to deity, provoking immediate concerns of blasphemy and the desire to stone Jesus. Similarly, Marshman inquires if Roy is conceding the point that before Christ became incarnate, he was in heaven. Shouldn't Roy deny that Christ had any existence before his birth? Marshman also maintains that the anthropomorphic language of ascent and descent does not affect the reality of the divine omnipresence. Indeed, in passages such as Genesis 11:5, where Yahweh "came down" to earth to view the tower of Babel, does this imply that there was no God remaining in heaven? Surely not. Lastly, the phrase "they have Moses" in Luke 16:29 referrs to the physical writings of Moses in the Pentateuch. As Jesus left no writings behind for his disciples, nor was he aware that gospels would later be composed, the more clear sense of Matthew 18:20 is that of the ubiquity of Christ.

Roy, in his *Final Appeal*, denies that the murderous intentions of the Jewish leaders necessarily implies that they understand the declaration of Jesus in John 8:58 as a blasphemous assertion of divinity, for they have already tried to stone him for healing on the Sabbath; they are continually angered by nearly every word and action of the Messiah. And even if they do misunderstand him as proclaiming equality with God, Jesus does not always correct people when they hold false opinions, such as him having a demon or being

6. Roy, "Second Appeal," 179.

7. Marshman, "Reply to 'A Second Appeal,'" 218.

a Samaritan. Roy adamantly reaffirms his denial of the ubiquity of Jesus: "It is not impossible for the omnipresent God that he should manifest himself wherever he chooses without violating his omnipresence; but the notion of occupying two very distant places at one time by a *son of man*, is, of course, contrary to the ideas acquired by human experience."[8]

MARSHMAN'S SECOND ARGUMENT: JESUS ASCRIBES TO HIMSELF A KNOWLEDGE AND AN INCOMPREHENSIBILITY OF NATURE EQUAL WITH AND PECULIAR TO GOD ALONE[9]

Marshman initiates his second argument by quoting Matthew 11:27, where Jesus declares that no one "knoweth the Son, but the Father; neither knoweth any man the Father, save the Son." The nature of the Son is as incomprehensible to humanity as that of the Father, and the Son has knowledge of the Father that is of the same quality the Father has of himself. Because of the divine knowledge that Jesus possesses, he beckons all who are weary to come to him, so that he can bestow rest (v. 28). Whose knowledge or power could issue such an invitation, if the speaker were not divine?

Roy objects to the assertion that incomprehensibility of nature is a peculiarly divine quality. Does Marshman mean *total* incomprehensibility of nature or does he mean impossibility of perfect knowledge? Surely he cannot be referring to the former, because God would thereby be completely cut off from human knowledge. If he means the latter, then it must be noted that the impossibility of perfect knowledge of the subject under investigation is not a quality distinctive to God alone, but also applies to plenty of items in nature. Facetiously, Roy remarks that no one knows "the day or hour" of the parousia, but this does not imply that the day is divine! He also points out that the ability to promise supernatural rest is not peculiar to Jesus in the Scriptures, but is promised by "all the prophets" who were "sent by the Almighty to afford mental rest to mankind, by imparting to them

---

8. Roy, "Final Appeal," 616–17.

9. The arguments are contained in Marshman, "Observations on Certain Ideas Contained in the Introduction to 'The Precepts of Jesus the Guide to Happiness and Peace,'" in *A Defence of the Deity and Atonement of Jesus Christ: In Reply to Ram-mohun Roy of Calcutta* (London: Kingsbury, Parbury, and Allen, 1822), 25; Roy, "Second Appeal," 180–82; Marshman, "Reply to 'A Second Appeal,'" 228–29; Roy, "Final Appeal," 626–28.

the comforts of divine revelation."[10] Surely Marshman does not think that these Old Testament promises of rest imply that the prophets themselves are divine or incarnations of God.

Marshman reaffirms that no created being can truly understand the infinite perfections of the Almighty. But Jesus declares that *he himself* can comprehend the nature of the Father; at the same time, he affirms that his own nature is *completely* incomprehensible to all save the Father. "Hence if he be a creature, he declares that the Father's nature is comprehensible *by a creature*, while he affirms that his own nature is comprehensible *by no creature*, but by God alone."[11] Jesus must either be equal in nature to the Father, or, more disturbingly, inferior in nature to the Father but blasphemously exalting his own finite nature. Such a blasphemer is assuredly not a trustworthy guide to "peace and happiness."

Roy replies by citing 1 John 3:1: "Therefore the world knoweth us not, because it knew him not." Such a forthright declaration of being misunderstood or unknown to the world does not raise the apostle up to the status of divinity or godlike incomprehensibility of nature. Roy prefers to paraphrase the meaning of Matthew 11:27 in this way: "No one but the Father can fully comprehend the object and extent of the Son's commission, and no one but the Son comprehends the counsels and designs of the Father with respect to the instruction and reformation of mankind."[12] In this interpretation, what was unknown to the world was the messianic identity and mission of Jesus; what Christ distinctively understood as the Messiah was the depth of the Father's commitment to uplift humanity.

MARSHMAN'S THIRD ARGUMENT: THE ACT OF FORGIVING SINS IN AN INDEPENDENT MANNER[13]

Marshman asserts that several times Jesus takes upon himself the divine prerogative of forgiving sins in the midst of theologically astute Jews, who would have rightly regarded such an act as blasphemous. In Mark 2:5–9, the

10. Roy, "Second Appeal," 182.

11. Marshman, "Reply to 'A Second Appeal,'" 228 (italics here and in quotes throughout this chapter are in the original).

12. Roy, "Final Appeal," 628.

13. The arguments are contained in Marshman, "Observations," 26; Roy, "Second Appeal," 182–84; Marshman, "Reply to 'A Second Appeal,'" 229–32; Roy, "Final Appeal," 629–31.

man with the withered hand is absolved of his sins by Jesus, and the religious officials immediately inquire who can forgive iniquities but God alone. Jesus does not defend himself by saying that he is forgiving in the name of God, as a prophet or messenger; instead, he displays almighty power by healing and asking if it is easier for him verbally to forgive or supernaturally to heal.

Roy responds by quoting the end of the parallel pericope, in Matthew 9:8: "they glorified God, which had given such power unto men." The crowd understands that Jesus, as a prophet, is as dependent on God for his abilities to forgive and heal as the Old Testament prophets were before him. Indeed, on the cross, Jesus petitions the Father to forgive those who have wronged him, rather than declaring forgiveness himself (Luke 23:34). Roy asserts, "The apostles, who witnessed the power of forgiving sins in the Savior, were thoroughly impressed with a belief that it was the Almighty Father who forgave sins through the Son."[14] It is God *himself* who exalts Jesus as the Messiah, so that through him, sinners can be called back into a relationship of reconciliation with the Father (Acts 5:31). If Jesus needs God to exalt him so that he can bestow the Father's mercy on others, in what sense can he be fully divine?

Marshman counters that in Matthew chapter 9, it is only in the opinion of the uneducated multitudes that Jesus is merely a prophet; however, in the minds of the scribes, who are the leading theologians, Jesus is committing an impious act by personally forgiving the man of his sins. They do not regard him as having a similar prophetic identity to Elijah or Moses, for if they had, they could not have so accused him. Jesus does not rebuke the charge of acting as an equal to God; rather, he enacts two further displays of divinity, by showing his omniscience in knowing their thoughts and by healing without reference to the name of God. With regard to the Acts 5:31 passage, when Roy inquires why a fully divine Jesus would have to be "exalted" by God, Marshman answers that the Father exalts Christ and restores Jesus' authority to forgive sins because he had voluntarily set aside his own glory in becoming human. As a result of this exaltation and restoration of authority, "whatever the Father doeth, these also the Son doeth likewise" (John 5:19). Furthermore, Marshman avers that Jesus himself "of his own will and pleasure forgives every sin which the Father is described as forgiving, the Father himself never forgiving one sin but in accordance with the *will* and intercession of the Son."[15]

14. Roy, "Second Appeal," 183.

15. Marshman, "Reply to 'A Second Appeal,'" 231.

Roy chides Marshman for suggesting that in Matthew 9:8 the phrase "who had given such power unto men" comes from the lips of the ignorant multitudes and, thereby, may be regarded as less than theologically correct. Rather, it was the evangelist Matthew himself, under divine inspiration, who penned the phrase as accurate theological commentary. Roy also reminds Marshman that the apostles had the power to forgive sins through Jesus, yet this does not make them divine. And the fact that the scribes were deeply offended by Christ is rendered less significant when one bears in mind that they were always looking for a pretext to destroy Jesus under the charge of blasphemy; they were similarly offended by a healing that took place on the Sabbath and by the raising of Lazarus. Roy draws his discussion to a close by quoting again from Acts 13:38, where the apostles understand that "through this *man*" is preached forgiveness of sins. To Roy, Jesus was a man who was given Messianic power by God to forgive the sins of those who were sincerely repentant.

MARSHMAN'S FOURTH ARGUMENT: THE ALMIGHTY POWER OF JESUS[16]

Marshman argues that Jesus repeatedly displayed acts of divine power and even ascribed to himself the ability to raise the dead. Jesus also declared that the Father had committed all judgment to him so "that all men should honour the Son, even as they honour the Father" (John 5:21–23). Marshman asks, "Can this language be reconciled to piety, sobriety, or truth, if Jesus did not intend to claim Divine honours as his proper right?"[17]

Roy responds that Jesus received the commission to judge from the Father: indeed, the key word in the John 5 passage is "committed." He believes that due attention must be given to context, where Jesus disavows equality with the Father: "the Son can do nothing of himself" (v. 19). Jesus instructs his followers to "believeth on him who sent me" (v. 24). Again, it is the *Father* who "hath given to the Son to have life in himself; and hath given him authority to execute judgment also" (vv. 26–27). Indeed, Jesus claims in verse 46 that Moses wrote of him, likely referring to the Deuteronomy 18:15–18 passage, which speaks of a prophet who will be raised up "like

16. The arguments are contained in Marshman, "Observations," 26–27; Roy, "Second Appeal," 184–89; Marshman, "Reply to 'A Second Appeal,'" 232–38; Roy, "Final Appeal," 632–39.

17. Marshman, "Observations," 27.

unto me." According to Roy, Jesus thought of himself as the Messiah or the prophet like unto Moses, but not divine. Jesus actually disclaims godlike omnipotence on many occasions: in Matthew 20:23, he states that to sit at his right hand or left hand is "not mine to give." Also, Matthew 12:28 asserts that Jesus cast out devils "by the spirit of God;" he is dependent upon God even in his ability to exorcise evil. The primary reason to honor Jesus in such passages as John 5:23 is that he is the Messiah, sent by the Father, and therefore worthy to be listened to and obeyed with respect to his commandments.

Marshman retorts that in the beginning of John 5, at the pool of Bethesda, Jesus has already claimed the prerogative of forgiving sins and then provides a display of omniscience and almighty healing power. Jesus then says that his Father is working, and therefore he works. John the evangelist comments that when Jesus called God his Father, this provoked the Jews, because he was "making himself equal with God" (vv. 17–18). Marshman asserts that John himself understood the implications of these matters. How can the Son do "whatsoever the Father does" if he is not equal with God? Even the highest archangel cannot claim such things. John goes on to write that the Father "showeth all things" to the Son (v. 20); what finite creature could understand such lofty matters? Jesus then adds that the Son "quickeneth whom he will" (v. 21), which is both a statement of almighty power and sovereign will. And then comes the stunning assertion that "all men should honour the Son as they honour the Father" (v. 23). This is why the Father judges no man but commits all judgment to the Son, so that Jesus will receive divine honor. Lastly, Marshman refers to Hebrews 3 for the New Testament perspective of the "Prophet like unto me," where Jesus is due much more glory and adoration than a merely human prophet such as Moses ever was.

Roy, in his *Final Appeal*, interrogates what exactly is meant by the Father's and Son's equality of nature:

> It is obvious, that one's calling another his Father, gives apparent ground to understand that there is an equality of nature or likeness of properties between them, either in quantity or quality of power in performing works. But to know what kind of equality or likeness should be meant in ch. 5: 18, we have luckily before us the following texts, in which Jesus declares, that his likeness with God consisted in doing what he saw the Father do, and quickening the

dead; avowing repeatedly, at the same time, his inferiority to and dependence on God.[18]

Roy queries why the Son should wait until the Father acts and then imitate, if the Father and Son are equally almighty? As to the question Marshman poses of how a finite being could understand all that God shows him, Roy retorts that God continually revealed to the prophets the divine secrets and mysteries. "Were they, in consequence, all infinite beings as the Editor [Marshman] argues, from this circumstance, Jesus is?"[19] In fact, Jesus exercised his power in a similar manner as the other prophets who were commissioned by God in their office. Roy introduces the argument, which he will develop later, that the Son can be "honored," in terms of respect and reverence, without being worshipped. He then quotes Galatians 4:14, where Paul says the Galatians received him as an angel of God, even as Christ Jesus. Roy asks: "Did Paul permit the Galatians to receive him with precisely the same kind of honour, both in kind and degree, as was due Christ Jesus?"[20] Neither does Jesus claim the same kind of honor as God the Father.

MARSHMAN'S FIFTH ARGUMENT: THE JUDGMENT OF THE WORLD BY JESUS[21]

The fact that God has committed the final judgment and the eternal destiny of countless millions to the hands of Jesus implies to Marshman that he must have the quality of omniscience. Not only the public actions, but also the private thoughts and deeds must be recollected and reviewed on the day of judgment. "One failure here, one circumstance overlooked, one feeling overrated, one action mistaken as to its motive, would at once tarnish the glory of the Divine Character and Government."[22] The weightiness of this pronouncement means that God must have entrusted this discrimination to no mere man.

Roy is not convinced by this argument; he once again emphasizes the Son's total dependence on the Father for administering such justice.

18. Roy, "Final Appeal," 632.

19. Ibid., 634.

20. Ibid., 637.

21. The arguments are contained in Marshman, "Observations," 27–29; Roy, "Second Appeal," 89–191; Marshman, "Reply to 'A Second Appeal,'" 238–39; Roy, "Final Appeal," 639–40.

22. Marshman, "Observations," 29.

Roy asserts that the Father is able "to bestow wisdom equal to the important nature of this office on the first-born of every creature, whom he has anointed and exalted even above his angels," referring here to the Messiah.[23] However, neither the Son nor the angels know the day and the hour of the judgment, but only the Father (Mark 13:32). Jesus thus has finite knowledge, not divine omniscient knowledge. John 5:27 makes clear that the Father "hath *given him authority* to execute judgment." And a few verses later, Jesus admits that "I can of my own self do nothing; as I hear, I judge; and my own judgment is just, because I seek not mine own will, but the will of the Father which hath sent me." Therefore, the authorization and ability to judge are given to the Messiah by the Father.

Marshman does not accept the concept of an omniscient creature or an all-knowing man; he asserts that such a person is a monster whose trace is not found in the Scriptures. Jeremiah 17:10 declares that it is God who searches the heart and gives to everyone a proper reward or rebuke; if Jesus acts as a universal judge, then he acts in a godlike manner. Marshman argues the following to prove that the divine Son's omniscience must be at work in the final discrimination of every individual's actions:

> To say, however, that the Father searches the heart for the Son, and having accurately judged of every man's ways and doings by examining his heart, communicates the result of the process to the Son, that he may appear the judge, though naturally incapable of making the previous examination, is directly to contradict our Lord's declaration, that the Father judgeth no man, as in this case the fact would really be, that the Son judgeth no man, but merely receives from the Father the result of his judging men's hearts.[24]

Roy counters that others in the Scriptures are "declared to be vested with the power of judging the world as well as the Son."[25] He is likely referring to the apostles whom Jesus promised would sit on twelve thrones to judge the twelve tribes of Israel at the restoration (Matt 19:28). Jesus exercises his right to judge in a similar manner as the *human* apostles he selected, who are endowed with wisdom by God and given permission to judge the twelve tribes. Roy acquiesces to the notion that the Son has life in himself and the power to judge, but this is always in relation to his office as the exalted Anointed One, and not as a divine being.

23. Roy, "Second Appeal," 190.
24. Marshman, "Reply to 'A Second Appeal,'" 238.
25. Roy, "Final Appeal," 640.

MARSHMAN'S SIXTH ARGUMENT:
WORSHIP IS ACCEPTED BY JESUS[26]

Marshman points out that in John's gospel (9:38), the blind man worships Jesus after having his sight restored, and Jesus is perfectly willing to permit this adoration. Matthew gives similar testimony to lepers (8:2) and mariners (14:33) worshipping Christ after seeing his miraculous signs. When tempted, Jesus retorts to Satan that only God is to be worshipped (Luke 4:8); yet on a number of occasions he permits himself to receive homage due to God alone. Marshman indicates that after his resurrection, Jesus declares that "all power" is delivered unto him; even Mohammed did not make such an audacious assertion. Marshman writes, "Could he [Mohammed] or any other mortal have managed the affairs of the world for a single day? Had he an arm like God? Could he thunder with a voice like this!"[27] Such omnipotent power to govern the world Jesus claims for himself.

Roy responds that "worship" can mean merely a token of civil respect due to superiors, as a mark of honor and acknowledgment of gratitude rather than adoration due to God. Daniel the prophet was perfectly willing to receive this sort of worship from King Nebuchadnezzar (Dan 2:46). In Jesus' own parable, he speaks of the servant falling down and worshipping his master in reverence (Matt 18:26). Roy asserts that respect is shown to Jesus by virtue of the fact that he is correctly identified as the Messiah and a prophet, not because he is a divine Son. Jesus does not accept worship that should be rendered to his Father alone, and he even rebukes the man who calls him "good" on the grounds that such an attribution is only appropriate to God. Indeed, Jesus repeatedly prays in humble submission to his heavenly Father and directs others to worship God. Roy argues that "the very act of prayer indeed implies an acknowledgment of inferiority to the being adored."[28]

Marshman grants that worship can imply civil respect. However, when the apostles worship Jesus after the resurrection, surely they are bestowing honor due only to Divinity. In fact, Thomas, in John 20:28, addresses the resurrected Jesus as "my Lord and my God." Stephen, in Acts 7:59, commits his dying, departing soul to the risen Lord Jesus. Furthermore, it is not what

26. The arguments are contained in Marshman, "Observations," 30–33; Roy, "Second Appeal," 191–97; Marshman, "Reply to 'A Second Appeal,'" 239–42; Roy, "Final Appeal," 640–44.

27. Marshman, "Observations," 32.

28. Roy, "Second Appeal," 195.

the common people know that matters, but what Jesus knows. If he permits himself to receive honor that is improper for a mere human to receive, then he is allowing his followers to fall into gross idolatry. With regard to Roy's query as to why Jesus always sought for his Father's glory, Marshman replies that Jesus willingly placed himself in a state of humiliation and kenosis; it was not appropriate for Christ to demand glorification during his years of ministry. Rather, it was the work of the Spirit to glorify the risen Son, and the Spirit led the apostles to worship him as God and Savior.

Roy reasserts that Jesus understands that those people are showing him civil respect. Thomas's expression "my Lord and my God" was a Semitic exclamation of wonder and astonishment common to Jews and Arabs after seeing something astounding, such as the nail prints in the hands of the risen Christ. Thomas does not say, "*You are* my Lord and my God." Finally, the singular command of Deuteronomy 6:13 ("Him *only* shalt thou worship and serve") is clearly and authoritatively repeated by Jesus in Matthew 4:10 and should be obeyed by all Christians who follow the Messiah.

MARSHMAN'S SEVENTH ARGUMENT: THE BAPTISMAL FORMULA[29]

Marshman lastly points to Jesus' adding his own name alongside the Father's in the sacred rite of baptism; this solemn act is a worshipful one where those baptized renounce all other false gods and pledge devotion to the true God. Jesus then reasserts his deity by adding that he will always be with the disciples, even until the end of the world. Did Moses, Abraham, or even Mohammed ever declare such godlike omnipresence, lasting until the consummation of all things?

Roy responds:

> A profession of belief in God is unquestionably common to all the religions supposed to have been founded upon the authority of the Old Testament; but each is distinguished from the other by a public profession of faith in their respective founders, expressing such a profession in a language that may clearly exhibit the

---

29. The arguments are contained in Marshman, "Observations," 33–34; Roy, "Second Appeal," 197–200; Marshman, "Reply to 'A Second Appeal,'" 242–48; Roy, "Final Appeal," 645–50.

inferior nature of those founders to the Divine Being, of whom they declare themselves the messengers.[30]

He quotes Exodus 14:31, where the people believed the Lord "and his servant Moses." Roy goes on to cite the declaration where Muslims include Mohammed in their statement of faith: "there is no God but Allah, and Mohammed is his Prophet." The mere association of a personal human name with a divine name in a profession of faith does not prove the divine identity of the prophet. In the baptismal formula, the inclusion of the name of Jesus was necessary to mark out the early Christian community from the Jews, who did not regard Jesus as the Messiah. Additionally, Mohammed made similar exalted assertions as Jesus' promise to be with his disciples until the end of the age. Roy quotes Mohammed as saying: "I was the first of all Prophets in creation; I was a Prophet when Adam was in earth and water; I am the Lord of those that were sent by God; my shadow is on the head only of my followers; he who has seen me, has seen God; he who has obeyed me has obeyed God."[31] Roy points out that such metaphorical expressions by Mohammed would be readily understood by Easterners as indicating the importance of his prophetic office, but similar metaphorical expressions by Jesus are misunderstood by Europeans as declarations of divinity.

Marshman discounts references from the Koran, since it is "pretending to be a Divine Revelation when it is not."[32] With regard to the Jews, they had no baptismal formula, and Moses is referred to in the Exodus 14 passage as God's "servant" to clearly indicate his inferior nature. Jesus, however, omits any clarifying phrase marking himself as subordinate to the Father in the baptismal formula. Additionally, in the Old Testament, circumcision was performed in no human name, and certainly not in the name of Moses. But baptism is performed in the name of the Son, Jesus. Marshman argues that the epithet "Son" does not imply inferiority, for why is a Son necessarily inferior to a Father in nature? Rather, the book of Revelation portrays an exalted picture of the Son, who sits on a throne and is due blessing, honor, glory, and power (5:13). And while Mohammed made many statements regarding his prophetic activity in the past, he never made a statement of abiding presence into the future ages, as did Christ.

Roy avers that it is proper in the baptismal formula to invoke the Son, who as the Messiah is the mediator of the covenant, in the same way that it

30. Roy, "Second Appeal," 197.

31. Ibid., 199.

32. Marshman, "Reply to 'A Second Appeal,'" 242.

is proper to invoke the Father as the divine object of worship and the Spirit as the conveyor of spiritual blessings. Regardless, the human messianic Son is still inferior in nature to the divine Father. Responding to Marshman's argument that there is no clarifying phrase of Jesus' subordination in the baptismal formula, Roy quotes 2 Chronicles 20:20, which commands belief in God and the prophets, but without the phrase "his servants" to indicate a subordinate role for the prophets. Even more pointedly, the Son directly declares himself in John 14:28 to be inferior to God the Father: "My Father is greater than I." Finally, for Roy, the future promise of an abiding presence "to the end of the age" refers to Jesus' perpetual influence and spiritual guidance, not to his eternal or omnipresent nature.

CONCLUSION

As Roy critiqued Marshman's seven arguments meant to demonstrate the divinity of Christ, there were several recurring themes and rhetorical strategies used by the Bengali Hindu reformer. He repeatedly drew attention to sections in the gospels that spoke of Christ's subordination and obedience in his earthy life to the Father. Even though Marshman argued that such passages indicated the voluntary kenosis of the divine Son during his incarnation, Roy instead interpreted them as admissions of Jesus' ultimate submission to the Father as a human rendering obeisance to God. As a Hindu who had been influenced by Islamic conceptions of monotheism, understanding and accepting the hierarchical roles within the Trinity would have been a major difficulty for Roy. Similarly, Roy continually argued that the supernatural abilities of Jesus, taken as proof of divinity by Marshman, were also shared at times by prophets and apostles who were dependent upon God for their powers. At the outset, Roy warned that supernatural feats would not be perceived as unique to Jesus in India, since there is no lack of such miraculous stories in the Hindu tradition. To someone raised in the Indian cultural context, Marshman's arguments accentuating the importance of Christ's special abilities might not be as singularly striking as they would to a European audience. Lastly, Roy interpreted many of the statements of the New Testament through his own Eastern cultural lens. When considering the exalted language Jesus used of himself and the worship he was willing to receive, Roy instinctively made comparisons with the hyperbole used by Mohammed in asserting his special status as a human Messenger of divine revelation and the common custom of showing "worshipful" respect to religious teachers throughout the Asian continent. Thus, it is useful to note the ways in which the Hindu-Islamic cultural framework of Roy heavily influenced his perception of Christ in the gospels and his reception of and response to Marshman's presentation of Jesus.

What Marshman did not emphasize in his seven arguments was the very thing that Roy found most touching and powerful: the teachings of Jesus. The compelling and challenging nature of Christ's instruction was not especially accentuated by Marshman. This is not surprising, since Marshman did not want Jesus to be placed alongside of other human religious teachers, diminishing his divine status. And perhaps Roy would have resorted to his usual line of argumentation that Jesus was a mere conduit of the Father's revelation, dependent upon God for the words of wisdom he uttered. Yet, there is a newness, a radicality, and a *scandalon* in the "precepts" of Christ that must have struck Roy as unprecedented in the Semitic and Indian traditions, given his high praise and admiration for the "guide to peace and happiness." It might have been beneficial for Marshman to demonstrate lucidly how in the teachings of Jesus, the new wine did indeed burst the old wineskins. By stoking the positive response and admiration that Roy had for the ethical instruction of Jesus, Marshman might have led Roy to a deeper consideration of the divine wisdom that uniquely permeated the discourses of Christ. Perhaps Roy eventually might have been open to seeing Jesus not simply as a human prophet or guru, but as something much more.

PART TWO

Adoniram Judson (1788–1850)

5

Adoniram Judson and Orlando Costas
American Baptist Missions over Two Centuries

ALLEN YEH

THIS CHAPTER IS A comparison of two historical figures from different times who have remarkable overlap in their biographical and spiritual journeys.[1] The men in question are Adoniram Judson (1788–1850) and Orlando Costas (1942–1987). At first glance, the two are quite different: one is white, the other is Latino. Though both counted the United States as home, one went East for missions while the other went South. One lived in the nineteenth century, the other lived in the twentieth.

Yet, there is far more that binds these two men than is immediately evident. Starting from the present may prove to be more illustrative than starting chronologically from the beginning. Today, if one were to walk into the famous Tabernacle Church in Salem, Massachusetts (one of the oldest Protestant churches in America), one would see in their Historical

1. This chapter was originally presented as a paper at the bicentennial celebration weekend of Adoniram Judson's sailing to Burma, February 17–19, 2012, which was hosted by the Boston Theological Institute's annual Orlando Costas Consultation on Global Mission, at the Tabernacle Church in Salem, Massachusetts. The theme of the 2012 Consultation was "American Culture and the Missionary Enterprise: Acknowledging the 200th Anniversary of the Judson Mission and the American Board of Commissioners for Foreign Missions." For a list of all the Costas Consultations that have taken place since its inception in 1990, see http://bostontheological.org/costasconsultation.html.

Room, among many other important artifacts and manuscripts, a singularly impressive piece of furniture: a long wooden bench, or missionary settee. It is the same wooden bench upon which sat Judson himself and four of his companions—Samuel Newell, Samuel Nott, Gordon Hall, and Luther Rice—as they were being commissioned to sail for Burma.[2] On the settee are four brass plaques, of which the second from the left and the one furthest to the right are of greatest concern to this chapter.

The two plaques are engraved as follows:

"Upon this seat Rev Messrs Newell, Judson, Nott, Hall & Rice sat in the Tabernacle Church, Salem—Feb 6, 1812—When ordained to the work of the Gospel Ministry as Missionaries to the Heathen in Asia"

"Upon this seat DR. ORLANDO E. COSTS [sic], ROSE COSTAS & CYNTHIA D. MOE sat in the Tabernacle Church, Salem—OCT 20, 1976—When commissioned as Missionaries of the U.C.B.W.M. to Costa Rica and Honduras"

The physical evidence that links Judson to Costas on this important piece of furniture is not coincidence. Orlando Costas was a student of history

2. Rosalie Hall Hunt, *Bless God and Take Courage: The Judson History and Legacy* (Valley Forge, PA: Judson Press, 2005), 31–32.

and specifically requested to be commissioned for the mission field on this settee because of its historical significance and because he saw some of that same pioneering spirit in himself. Why would Costas choose to follow in the footsteps of Judson, of all people?

The first and most obvious point of comparison is their calling as missionaries. Both felt compelled by God to devote their lives to overseas service, but both men died young of disease that ravaged their bodies—Judson when he was 61 years old, on April 12, 1850,[3] and Costas when he was 45 years old, on November 5, 1987.[4] Yet, both accomplished extraordinary things in the course of their lives.

Both men were practitioners and scholars. Missions and missiology are necessarily integrative disciplines that require high physical, mental, and spiritual capacities. This is due to the rigors of living overseas, the challenges of adapting to another culture and climate, the facility needed not only to learn a foreign language but to translate the Bible and literature into that language, and the constant combating of disease and personal enemies, whether human or supernatural.

Academically, Adoniram Judson was trained at some of the finest schools of his day—Brown University for his undergraduate education, followed by ministerial training at Andover Theological Seminary. His academic achievements were even more impressive on the mission field: he completed a Burmese Bible, grammar, and dictionary.[5] Orlando Costas earned four degrees, including an undergraduate degree from the Inter-American University in Puerto Rico, two Masters degrees from Winona Lake School of Theology and Garrett-Evangelical Theological Seminary, and a doctorate of theology (D.Theol.) at the Free University of Amsterdam. He also was the author of ten books (half in English and half in Spanish), as well as hundreds of journal articles and chapters in books.

Costas was not only physically linked to Judson because of the plaques on the missionary settee but through his job at Andover Newton Theological School (ANTS), which was the modern-day heir to Judson's Andover Seminary.[6] Orlando Costas was appointed to a chair, fittingly

3. Hunt, *Bless God*, 235. It was a severe cold, dysentery, and a high fever that eventually took Judson's life.

4. See *Christianity Today*, News, December 11, 1987. A prolonged bout with stomach cancer ended Costas's life.

5. Hunt, *Bless God*, 343.

6. Andover Newton Theological School is not Andover Theological Seminary's physical heir, as the private high school Phillips Academy Andover now stands on that

as the Adoniram Judson professor of missiology at Andover Newton. He later became ANTS's dean, making Costas the first ethnic minority dean of any mainline Protestant seminary in the United States.[7] Adoniram Judson also has a "first" claim: he is the first intercontinental missionary from America's shores.[8] Together, these groundbreaking pioneers of the missions field and academia have blazed trails for others to follow and not for personal glory.

Their New England upbringing and training alludes to a focus on universities and students. Boston has perhaps the highest number of universities per capita of any city in the United States. It is not surprising, therefore, that these men were so involved in student movements of missions. Judson received his missionary impetus from "The Brethren," six students at Williams College in western Massachusetts in 1806, who met together under a haystack to start the American missionary impulse. Four of them, Samuel Mills, James Richards, Samuel Nott, and Samuel Newell (the latter two are pictured in the commissioning sketch with Judson above) who enrolled with Judson at Andover Seminary.[9] In fact, today if you go on the campus of Phillips Academy Andover, there is a boulder, dubbed "Missionary Rock," on the shores of the on-campus pond, engraved with the words:

---

site, but ANTS is Andover Seminary's institutional successor.

7. "Orlando E. Costas 1942–1987," *Today's Ministry* 5, no. 2 (Winter 1988) 3.

8. Judson is not the first overseas missionary from America, as that would be George Leile going to Jamaica in 1782, as explained in chapter 8 of this book; but even Leile cannot claim to be the first American missionary, as the claim belongs to John Eliot, the "Apostle to the Indians," who was a domestic, though cross-cultural, missionary to the Algonquin Indians in the latter half of the seventeenth century. Eliot translated the Bible into the Massachusett language, thus producing the first Bible ever published on American soil.

9. Hunt, *Bless God*, 17.

Interestingly, most students on Phillips Academy's campus are unaware of this rock's existence or the launching of the student missionary movement from their doorstep.

> In the missionary woods once extending to this spot, the first missionary students of Andover Seminary walked and talked one hundred years ago, and on this secluded knoll met to pray. In memory of these men Adoniram Judson, Samuel Nott, Samuel J. Mills, Samuel Newell, Gordon Hall, James Richards, Luther Rice, whose consecrated purpose to carry the Gospel to the heathen world led to the formation of the first American Society for Foreign Missions. In recognition of the two hundred and forty-eight missionaries trained in Andover Seminary, and in gratitude to Almighty God, this stone is set up in the Centennial year of the American Board 1910

Interestingly, 1910 was the very same year of the famous Edinburgh 1910 World Missionary Conference where organizer and missionary statesman John R. Mott rallied students from the YMCA, the Student Volunteer Movement, and other organizations, with the famous watchword: "The Evangelization of the World in this Generation."[10] So one hundred years

10. Brian Stanley, *World Missionary Conference, Edinburgh 1910* (Grand Rapids: Eerdmans, 2009), 88.

after Judson, his legacy and the legacy of other students obviously made an impact on missionary history when you see the amount of student involvement that was present at Edinburgh 1910. Today, students continue to be involved in world missions, as evidenced by events such as InterVarsity's triennial Urbana student missions conference, and even the commissioning of students at this event on the two-hundredth anniversary of Judson's sailing for Burma.[11] Orlando Costas would later have his own mark on Edinburgh 1910's history, as he was a speaker at the seventy-fifth anniversary of that historical event, Edinburgh 1985, sponsored by the Student Christian Movement (SCM).[12] Though Edinburgh 1910 is often considered "the birthplace of the ecumenical movement,"[13] that may be a bit of a misnomer. It was seriously undeserving, in some regards, to deserve that name, perhaps most glaringly in the area of non-Western representation: "the conference was a gathering of mission executives and missionaries; indigenous Christians were a dubious luxury whose presence was not integral to the character of the event."[14] In an attempt at reparation, the organizers of the 1985 Edinburgh SCM conference invited only Two-Thirds World speakers, effectively turning the original event on its head: two from Africa, Mercy Oduyoye of Nigeria and Leonardo Appies of South Africa, two from Asia, Annathaia Abayasekera of Sri Lanka and Kosuke Koyama of Japan, and two

11. In fact, immediately after this paper was delivered at the Tabernacle Church in Salem, the students in attendance at the Costas Consultation, mostly from the Boston Theological Institute, gathered around the famous missionary settee bench, and all the faculty gathered around them and prayed for them to "commission" them to missions for the future. So really, there ought to be a fifth brass plaque engraved on the bench today!

12. "The Student Christian Movement came into being in 1889 as a loose network of students dedicated to missionary work overseas. It rapidly broadened its aims and membership to become the largest student organisation in Britain. . . . SCM was instrumental in bringing about the Edinburgh Conference in 1910. The conference marked the beginnings of the modern ecumenical movement, and also played a vital role in the formation of the British and World Council of Churches." "History of SCM," on the Student Christian Movement's website: http://www.movement.org.uk/about-us/history.

13. Marlin VanElderen, *Introducing the World Council of Churches* (Geneva: WCC, 1990), 17.

14. Brian Stanley, "Edinburgh 1910 and the *Oikoumene*," in *Ecumenism and History: Studies in Honour of John H. Y. Briggs*, ed. Anthony R. Cross (Carlisle, UK: Paternoster, 2002), 93. Stanley also mentions that only seventeen non-Western delegates were present, and all were from Asia (eight Indians, four Japanese, three Chinese, one Korean, and one Burmese). There were only two black Africans present, both as non-delegates, and not a single representative from Latin America. Beyond the lack of non-Western representation, there were also no Roman Catholics present.

from Latin America, Enrique Dussel of Argentina[15] and of course Orlando Costas of Puerto Rico. The moderator of the event was Emilio Castro, then the General Secretary of the WCC.[16] Costas's address was entitled "Mission in a New Age" and his words tackle these issues directly:

> This is indeed a historic occasion for Enrique Dussell and I. We are, after all, both Latin Americans, from two extremes of the continent, he from Argentina and I from Puerto Rico. We represent a continent that was left out of Edinburgh 1910, as Emilio Castro reminded us the other night. We represent the bone of contention of Edinburgh 1910. Enrique Dussell is a Roman Catholic. And those of you who have read the story of Edinburgh 1910, you will recall it was in deference to the Roman Catholics that the Anglo Catholics insisted that Latin America (or, South America as is usually called in the British Isles), should not be present. But I am a Protestant of evangelical stock; I represent those who insisted in the nineteenth century, and still speak in this day, that Latin America is far from being an evangelized land. Enrique Dussell and I stand as two representatives of ecumenical Christians in Latin America. For now we know that indeed Latin America may have been Christianized, but it has yet to be fully evangelized. So this is a historic moment, that you should have a Roman Catholic and an evangelical representing the outsiders of Edinburgh 1910. And we are here to bear witness to the gospel, we are here to let you know that a lot has happened since 1910, we are here to speak on behalf of our sisters and brothers, and we are here united as women and men who have new visions and are hearing a new call for mission in a new age.[17]

Being early facilitators of World Christianity is another similarity between these two men. Judson opened up Southeast Asia for other missionaries, but more importantly was well ahead of his time in training Burmese nationals to preach the gospel to their own people. He realized that the mission is most sustainable in this way.[18] Andover Newton, in honor of Costas's memory, set up a memorial fund in his honor after his

---

15. Dussel is considered by many to be the premiere Catholic Latin American church historian alive today.

16. Information and audio tapes of the speakers' addresses courtesy of Rev. Robert Anderson at World Exchange in Edinburgh.

17. Orlando Costas, "Mission in a New Age," address given at the Edinburgh 1985 Student Christian Movement conference, audio tape transcribed by Allen Yeh.

18. Hunt, *Bless God*, 343.

death called the Orlando E. Costas Hispanic and Latin American Ministries Program. The purpose of this fund is to encourage multiculturalism and the training of Hispanic ministers at ANTS, especially with the recognition that Hispanics are the fastest-growing minority group in the United States.[19] It was Costas who provided the template and vision for empowering and training Hispanics in the United States. These two trends match the two faces of World Christianity: what Philip Jenkins calls "The Next Christendom"[20]—the shift of the center of gravity of Christianity to the Two-Thirds World; and what Soong-Chan Rah calls "The Next Evangelicalism"[21]—the shift of the center of gravity of Christianity in the United States to ethnic minorities and immigrants.

Their missionary work of course is paramount. Adoniram Judson came to a Christian-less Burma in 1813, and a century later the country had over 100,000 believers.[22] In contrast to William Carey, who was involved a variety of missional endeavors, Judson was primarily concerned with evangelism, and the results bore much fruit.[23] For Orlando Costas, his calling was as more of an academic than a straight evangelist. He went to Costa Rica to become a professor of homiletics and the chairman of the department of evangelism of the *Seminario Bíblico Latinoamericano*, the flagship seminary of Latin America Mission (LAM), in San José.[24] But beyond his academic work, he was a key figure with LAM's successful ministry, Evangelism In-Depth,[25] which was a continent-wide network of evangelistic efforts that took him throughout all of Latin America.[26] Whereas Costas reached Latin America with open-air evangelistic marches, Judson reached Burma with contextualized Burmese preaching through *zayats*, or

19. "Memorial Fund to Develop Costas' Vision," *Today's Ministry* 5, no. 2 (Winter 1988) 1, 3.

20. Philip Jenkins, *The Next Christendom: The Coming of Global Christianity* (Oxford: Oxford University Press, 2002).

21. Soong-Chan Rah, *The Next Evangelicalism: Releasing the Church from Western Cultural Captivity* (Downers Grove, IL: InterVarsity, 2009).

22. Hunt, *Bless God*, 347.

23. Ruth Tucker, *From Jerusalem to Irian Jaya: A Biographical History of Christian Missions* (Grand Rapids: Zondervan, 2004), 139.

24. Nancy Freund, "Costas to 'Invade' Costa Rica Soon," *Milwaukee Sentinel*, December 20, 1969, 5.

25. Tucker, *From Jerusalem*, 448.

26. Paul E. Pretiz and W. Dayton Roberts, *"Like a Mighty Army": R. Kenneth Strachan and the Global March of Evangelism-in-Depth* (Miami: Latin America Mission, 1998).

Buddhist roadside shelters.[27] Strategically effective missions came naturally to both men.

Part of the reason for their missionary impulse was their denominational allegiance. Adoniram Judson was sent out for mission with the Congregationalists but became a Baptist on the sea voyage to Asia through his examination of the Bible. His theological convictions would not let him go, as he recounted:

> My change of sentiments on the subject of baptism is considered by my missionary brethren as incompatible with my continuing as their fellow-laborer in the mission which they contemplate. . . . The dissolution of my connection with the Board of Commissioners, and a separation from my dear missionary brethren, I consider most distressing consequences of my late change of sentiments. . . . I have now the prospect before me of going alone to some distant island, unconnected with any society at present existing, from which I might be furnished with . . . pecuniary support.[28]

Orlando Costas likewise switched from the Congregationalists to the Baptists, but due more to political than theological reasons. He wrote:

> I came to the American Baptist Churches via the Puerto Rican Baptist Convention, which is, paradoxically, one of its regional components. (Paradoxically, because Puerto Rico is not a state of the Union, but rather a colonial territory, even though this is denied by the U.S. government.)[29]

Interestingly, for Judson, becoming a Baptist was a frightening prospect because it entailed being a nonconformist and without financial or moral support. For Costas, becoming a Baptist was emboldening because it represented freedom to him: it was emblematic of political independence and autonomy, which in turn symbolized religious freedom. Nevertheless, being a Baptist made missions a natural fit for both men. The Baptist World Alliance recently described themselves to the worldwide Anglican communion as follows:

> Baptists are a missionary people. Since their beginnings 400 years ago, they have spread the good news of Jesus Christ throughout

27. Tucker, *From Jerusalem*, 135.

28. Orlando Costas, "Ecumenical Experiences of an Hispanic Baptist," *Journal of Ecumenical Studies* 17, no. 2 (Spring 1980) 119–20. "The Board of Commissioners" here refers to the American Board of Commissioners for Foreign Missions (ABCFM).

29. Ibid.

the world, together with their particular way of living out the Christian faith. Baptists brought significant leadership to the modern missionary movement, especially through the pioneering work of William Carey in India, Adoniram Judson in Myanmar, George Lisle in Jamaica, Johann Gerhard Oncken in continental Europe, Alfred Saker in Cameroon, William Buck Bagby in Brazil and George Grenfell in the Democratic Republic of Congo.[30]

It is no surprise, then, that a Baptist, William Carey, is considered the father of modern missions; that the American Baptists call their publishing house Judson Press; that renowned missionary Lottie Moon is considered the patron saint of Southern Baptists; or that the Southern Baptist Convention recently "adopted an informal, non-legal 'Great Commission Baptists' descriptor, to be used by any church that wishes to use it."[31] So it was with Judson and Costas: their Baptist hearts were none other than missionary hearts. "Baptize" is one of the key verbs of the Great Commission, and the evangelistic impulse leads to the initiating act of the Christian life: baptism.

Music was another area that touched both men, showing that their reach went beyond just the intellectual and ministerial to even the creative arts. Judson wrote the first-ever Christian hymns in Burmese, including his most famous, "Come Holy Spirit, Dove Divine."[32] Costas, on the other hand, was not a composer but a performer. He was endowed with a marvelous singing voice, which he used often in the early years of his ministry, especially in forming a musical trio with two of his friends.[33]

Finally, what must not be neglected is the role of the wives of these two men. Ann Judson and Rose Costas were indispensable to the successful mission and well-being of Adoniram and Orlando, providing much-needed partnership not only in the missionary task, but also in companionship, friendship, and spiritual strength. Though this chapter is focused primarily on Adoniram and Orlando, to fail to mention their wives would be to forget

30. *Conversations Around the World 2000–2005: The Report of the International Conversations between the Anglican Communion and the Baptist World Alliance* (London: Anglican Communion Office, 2005), 17.

31. Erin Roach, "'Great Commission' Descriptor Approved by Messengers," *Baptist Press*, June 19, 2012.

32. Hunt, *Bless God*, 345.

33. Orlando Costas, "Conversion as a Complex Experience," in *Down to Earth: Studies in Christianity and Culture; The Papers of the Lausanne Consultation of Gospel and Culture*, ed. John R. W. Stott and Robert Coote (Grand Rapids: Eerdmans, 1980), 175. Costas was first encouraged in this endeavor by the Police Athletic League Talent Theater Group, and was even awarded a scholarship to study with a voice coach in New York.

that the two shall be of "one flesh." Therefore Ann and Rose are definitely not second-class citizens, not only in their identity but also in terms of what they contributed to the ministry.[34]

34. It is unfortunate that Ann's name is not written on the brass plaque on the missionary settee as Rose's was, but partially that had to do with the time in which the Judsons lived, when women were not recognized as equal partners.

6

From the Judsons to Global Christianity, 1812–2012

Todd M. Johnson

It might be tempting, from the vantage point of the two hundredth commissioning anniversary of the first ordained American foreign missionaries, including Adoniram and Ann Judson, to directly attribute the remarkable spread of Christianity around the world to these and other missionaries' courageous obedience to the Great Commission.[1] Even limiting the scope of their influence to Burma—the Judsons' primary place of overseas service—their commendable work would produce a very incomplete, and potentially misleading, explanation for the growth of Christianity around the world from 1812 to 2012. In fact, between the Judsons then and us today lies a vast assemblage of unsung local believers around the world who spread the gospel without fanfare or recognition.

1. An earlier version of this article was prepared for the two hundredth anniversary of the ordination of the first missionaries sent out by the American Board of Commissioners of Foreign Missions held at Tabernacle Church in Salem, Massachusetts, on February 6, 2012. A series of commemorative meetings were held in and around Salem from February 5 through February 20, 2012. For more details, see "American Culture and the Missionary Enterprise: Acknowledging the 200th Anniversary of the Judson Mission and the American Board of Commissioners for Foreign Missions, February 2012," Boston Theological Institute (Newton Centre, MA), online: http://www.boston-theological.org/judson200.html.

Nonetheless, the Judsons were an essential initial catalyst in the introduction of the gospel to Burma.[2]

THE JUDSONS' WORLD IN 1812

Born August 9, 1788, in Malden, Massachusetts, Adoniram Judson entered the world as the son of a pastor in an environment in which churches were mired in theological divisions between conservatives and liberals. His father was a conservative Congregationalist pastor who sparred with liberals in several of his congregations, sometimes resulting in his ejection. This explains why the young Judson lived in so many different places around the Boston area.[3]

The Judson family moved to Wenham on January 10, 1793. The town paid the elder Judson a salary of just over three hundred dollars a year but did not give him a raise for the entire six years he served there. A few short miles away lay maritime Salem, one of the wealthiest cities in the world,[4] with the smell of imported spices apparent from well outside the city limits. At age eleven, the youthful Judson was studying marine navigation from one of the leading navigators in the United States. Courtney Anderson observes, "To a poor country minister and his wide-eyed young son, Salem Harbor must have seemed like a cornucopia from which poured all the riches of the Orient."[5] Manasseh Cutler, pastor at nearby First Congregational Church in Hamilton, likely suggested this course of study for young Judson. Cutler practiced medicine, inoculated people against smallpox, measured the distance of the stars with sextant and telescope, studied Jupiter's moons, made botanical investigations, and did a good deal of work

---

2. Advocates of leaving evangelism to the "nationals" should note that today thousands of people groups still have no "national" Christians. The essence of missions is that someone must cross an ethnic, cultural, or linguistic barrier to spread the gospel beyond its current boundaries. The Judsons were one such couple in 1812.

3. See Courtney Anderson, *To the Golden Shore: The Life of Adoniram Judson* (Garden City, NY: Doubleday, 1961), the classic biography of Judson, from which these reflections are drawn. While there are many more recent critical works, Anderson still stands out as a readable and accessible account of the events in Judson's life and ministry.

4. See Robert Booth, *Death of an Empire: The Rise and Murderous Fall of Salem, America's Richest City* (New York: St. Martin's, 2011). When shipping magnate E. Hasket Derby died in 1799, he had a combined net worth of $31.4 billion (adjusted for today's rates), making him one of the seventy-five richest men who ever lived.

5. Anderson, *To the Golden Shore*, 34.

with the microscope—then an almost-unheard-of instrument of science. No doubt Judson's studies in Salem gave him an important global context for future decisions regarding vocation.

Though his parents hoped he would become a minister, Judson had other plans. While attending what would later become Brown University in Providence, Rhode Island, he became a practical deist, turned his back on expectations that he would join the ministry, and later went to New York City to work in theater. This proved less than practical, and while on the journey back to Massachusetts, he experienced a crisis of faith. Judson providentially spent the night at an inn where he overheard a man dying in hopelessness and agony in the next room. When he inquired in the morning, the deceased turned out to be his deist mentor from Brown. This set him back on the journey to ministry, but when he was later admitted to the new seminary in Andover—established as a conservative alternative to Harvard—Judson was not a believer. Nonetheless, his professors saw great potential in him, and they would not be disappointed.

Judson continued to develop his love for distant places while at seminary. Although ridiculed there for his newfound desire to be a foreign missionary, Judson read everything he could find related to Asia. This included *An Account of an Embassy to the Kingdom of Ava*, written by British Army officer Michael Symes. The book begins, "There are no countries on the habitable globe, where the arts of civilized life are understood, of which we have so limited a knowledge as those that lie between the British possessions in India and the empire of Burma."[6] Judson was attracted to Burma by this challenge.

It was on a snowy day in February of 1810 that Judson finally committed to be a foreign missionary. He wrote in his journal:

> It was during a solitary walk in the woods behind the college, while meditating and praying on the subject, and feeling half inclined to give it up, that the command of Christ, "Go into all the world and preach the Gospel to every creature," was presented to my mind with such clearness and power, that I came to a full decision, and through great difficulties appeared in my way, resolved to obey the command at all events.[7]

Shortly after this, Judson was offered the prestigious position of assistant to the pastor at Park Street Church in downtown Boston. When he

6. Anderson, *To the Golden Shore*, 66.

7. Anderson, *To the Golden Shore*, 68.

declined and explained his call to foreign missions to his family, they broke down into uncontrollable sobbing. Why, they wondered, should he waste his life half a world away where he would not be appreciated?

Judson would not have to face his uncertain future alone, however. Unknown to him, several other students at Andover Theological Seminary were privately committed to foreign missions, as he was. They came together in a secret group called "The Society of the Brethren," whose stated goal was that "each member shall keep himself absolutely free from every engagement which, after his prayerful attention, and after consultation with his brethren, shall be deemed incompatible with the object of this society, and shall hold himself in readiness to go on a mission when and where duty may call."[8] This group was essential for those young men to keep and nurture their nascent vision.

The next step for these young enthusiasts was the formation of a missionary-sending society, for which they needed the support of their elders. One key figure was Samuel Worchester, the pastor of Tabernacle Church in Salem. He had delivered a historic missionary sermon the previous year to the Massachusetts Missionary Society. After hearing the appeal of the students to create a missionary-sending society in 1810, Worchester and others argued among themselves as to whether the idea was feasible. In the end they decided, "We had better not attempt to stop God."[9] This marked the founding of the American Board of Commissioners for Foreign Missions, the first foreign missionary–sending institution in the United States.[10]

In the meantime, Judson fell in love with Ann Hasseltine of Bradford, who, on her own, also had come to a decision to give her life to serving God in distant places. She, too, spent some time in Salem and probably there picked up an interest in the world outside New England. However, her father had to be convinced to allow his daughter to embark on such a dangerous missionary life. Judson's letter to Mr. Hasseltine is telling of the discourse surrounding this issue:

> I have now to ask, whether you can consent to part with your daughter early next spring, to see her no more in this world; whether you can consent to her departure, and her subjection to

8. Anderson, *To the Golden Shore*, 72.

9. Anderson, *To the Golden Shore*, 77.

10. For an excellent full-length treatment of the ABCFM, see Clifford Putney and Paul T. Burlin, eds., *The Role of the American Board in the World: Bicentennial Reflections on the Organization's Missionary Work, 1810–2010* (Eugene, OR: Wipf & Stock, 2012).

> the hardships and sufferings of a missionary life; whether you can consent to her exposure to the dangers of the ocean; to the fatal influence of the southern climate of India [Judson's first destination]; to every kind of want and distress; to degradation, insult, persecution, and perhaps a violent death.[11]

One of Mr. Hasseltine's kin responded for Ann's father when he declared stoutly that he would tie his own daughter to the bedpost rather than let her go on such a harebrained venture. Despite this, Mr. Hasseltine left it to his daughter to decide. She went to nearby Beverly to seek advice from a trusted mentor, where the focus was on whether or not God was leading her to go. Her reply to Judson was in the positive, but she emphasized, "nor were my determinations formed in consequence of an attachment to an earthly object; but with a sense of obligations to God, and with a full conviction of its being a call in providence, and consequently my duty."[12]

Meanwhile, the American Board was having trouble raising funds. They decided to send Judson to the London Missionary Society (LMS) to see if an arrangement could be made whereby the American Board would supply missionaries who would be funded—but not controlled by—the LMS. Judson's trip was a success in the sense that the LMS agreed to take on the missionaries financially, but they would not relinquish on-the-field oversight of the missionaries to the newly formed American society. While Judson was in London, however, a large bequest from a wealthy American was given to the American Board. Nonetheless, when the American Board met in September 1811, they decided not to send any missionaries for the time being because an embargo held up maritime trade and made future business prospects in Asia dim. In protest, Judson threatened to go to London immediately to become an LMS missionary, but the Board relented and began making plans to send the missionaries abroad.

The process culminated with a cascade of events in February 1812. The young missionaries were scheduled to leave on February 10. Adoniram Judson and Ann Hasseltine were married on Wednesday, February 5, in Haverhill, Massachusetts. On Thursday, February 6, fifteen hundred people attended the ordination service of the missionaries at Tabernacle Church in Salem. The evening service on Sunday, February 9, was also packed with supporters of the young missionaries. The sailing was delayed until Wednesday, February 19, due to bad weather. The trip to India took almost

11. Anderson, *To the Golden Shore*, 92.

12. Anderson, *To the Golden Shore*, 93.

four months, and as they arrived, they saw what they thought was their first Hindu, who turned out to be a Muslim. Another year would pass before the Judsons finally arrived in Burma.

THE WORLD IN 2012

Events over the past two hundred years have transported us to a world radically different than that of the Judsons. When they sailed out of Salem Harbor in 1812, twenty percent of the world was Christian and over ninety percent of all Christians were Europeans. In 2012, the world is about thirty-three percent Christian, and only about twenty-five percent of all Christians worldwide are Europeans.[13] In the intervening period, Christianity grew rapidly in Africa (mainly through conversions) and Latin America (mainly because of high birth rates), while declining in Europe (mainly through defections and low birth rates).[14]

Christianity has taken firm root in Asia, including significant minorities in China and India. In the past one hundred years, unexpected stories of church growth have been found in the Korean peninsula (1907 to present), China (1970s), Nepal (1990s), and Mongolia and Cambodia (2000s). Burma itself saw a significant increase of Christians. In 1812 there were very few Christians in Burma, but today there are over four million Christians there (about eight percent of the population).[15] Despite such growth, however, the continent remains home to vast non-Christian populations. Asians were unprepared for the wave of atheism and agnosticism that accompanied the rise of communism in the twentieth century. But sixty years on, a resurgence of religion is pushing down the number of atheists and agnostics, while traditionally Asian religions, such as Buddhism, Daoism, and Chinese folk-religion, are experiencing a revival in both numbers and influence.

In 1812 over ninety-nine percent of the world's population was religious, but by 2012 this had fallen to below eighty-nine percent. Such a

13. The facts and figures presented here are found in Todd M. Johnson and Kenneth R. Ross, eds., *Atlas of Global Christianity* (Edinburgh: Edinburgh University Press, 2009). While this book covers mainly the 1910–2010 period, figures for 1810 were added from the *World Christian Database* (Leiden: Brill, 2012) for the two hundred–year timeline. See the *World Christian Database* online: http://www.worldchristiandatabase.org/.

14. Johnson and Ross, *Atlas*, 62–65.

15. A detailed narrative and demographic history of Christianity in Myanmar (Burma) is found in David B. Barrett, George T. Kurian, and Todd M. Johnson, eds., *World Christian Encyclopedia*, 2nd ed. (New York: Oxford University Press, 2001), 517–21.

general analysis, however, hides the fact that the high point for the world's nonreligious population was around 1970, when almost twenty percent of the world's population was either agnostic or atheist. The collapse of communism in the late twentieth century means that the world is more religious in 2012 than in 1970.[16] In this way, our world more closely resembles that of the Judsons.

Given this mix of similarities and differences, how did we get from 1812 to 2012—from the Judsons to global Christianity?

Looking at the history of Christianity in Burma provides some important clues. The gospel was effectively spread there by what is now termed "indigenous agency."[17] This method emerged during Judson's lifetime but was largely unrecognized at the time. The primary carriers of the gospel message were to a great extent unknown individual converts from among the indigenous people the missionaries set out to reach. In Judson's case, it was an untrustworthy thief who was most effective in spreading the gospel beyond the narrow confines of the missionary community, who focused largely on evangelizing the majority power-holders, the Burmese. It was the "wild" Karen who responded to the gospel, however—a jungle tribe that had to knock incessantly on the missionaries' door to get their attention.[18]

Even so, the missionaries did make some important strategic decisions in their approach that set the stage for the later indigenization of Christianity. In Burma they took a very different approach to "primitive" tribes than their fellow missionaries did to Native Americans in America. Bible translations were slow to appear among Native Americans, but within a few decades there were already two full Bible translations in Burma, including Judson's Burmese Bible. As missiologists Lamin Sanneh and Andrew Walls have shown, this principle of translation eventually changed the balance of power among peoples who embraced Christianity.[19] Between the

16. Johnson and Ross, *Atlas*, 28–31.

17. Robert E. Frykenberg writes, "Thus there can be no easy summary of the relations between missions and colonialism. Hitherto there has been too much emphasis on linkages and too little attention paid to indigenous agency, impacts of conversion, reactions to conversion (or to counter-conversion), and indigenous movements. Much of what really happened still lies hidden from the gaze of historians." Frykenberg, "Christian Missions and the Raj," in *Missions and Empire*, ed. Norman Etherington (Oxford: Oxford University Press, 2005), 129.

18. Anderson, *To the Golden Shore*, 389.

19. See Lamin Sanneh, *Translating the Message: The Missionary Impact on Culture* (Maryknoll, NY: Orbis, 1989) and Andrew F. Walls, *The Missionary Movement in Christian History: Studies in the Transmission of Faith* (Maryknoll, NY: Orbis, 1996).

"translation principle" and "indigenous agency," the kind of Christianity that spread in Burma quickly differentiated itself from that of the colonial missionaries. In essence, foreign missionaries in Burma provided the necessary spark while local evangelists did the work on the ground, producing a culturally relevant version of the Christian faith.

SIMILARITIES AFTER TWO CENTURIES

Today we face many challenges similar to those faced by the Judsons, such as whether or not we will sacrifice our personal plans for the sake of a larger vision of reaching the world for Christ. A central characteristic of both ages is courage. Deciding to live among peoples previously unreached with the gospel requires courage and faith, no matter where that might be. In fact, it is a rare individual who is willing to give up life, home, and liberty for the sake of others. Surprisingly, Christian family and friends in our globalized world still greet such aspirations with incredulity, despair, and even ridicule.

The struggle between Christians with differing theological and social perspectives has intensified. Hundreds of Christian denominations in 1812 have mushroomed into tens of thousands in 2012.[20] Today, more than ever, we are challenged to work together rather than compete. In particular, Protestants face the proliferation of independent churches in Africa, Asia, and Latin America, as well as in the Western world.

Recent research reveals that as many as eighty-six percent of all Muslims, Hindus, and Buddhists do not personally know a Christian.[21] This must be viewed negatively in light of the strong biblical theme of incarnational witness that is at the heart of Christianity. Christians should know, live among, and love their neighbors! In the twenty-first century it is important to realize that the responsibility for reaching adherents of other religions is too large for the missionary enterprise. While missionaries will always be at the forefront of innovative strategies, the whole church needs to participate in inviting people of other faiths to consider Jesus Christ.

20. See Todd M. Johnson et al., "Christianity 2012: The 200th Anniversary of American Foreign Missions," *International Bulletin of Missionary Research* 36, no. 1 (January 2012) 28–29. The number was estimated at five hundred in 1800, grew to forty-three thousand by mid-2012, and is expected to increase to fifty-five thousand by 2025.

21. For complete results and methodology, see Todd M. Johnson and Charles L. Tieszen, "Personal Contact: The *Sine Qua Non* of Twenty-First Century Christian Mission," *Evangelical Missions Quarterly* 43, no. 4 (October 2007) 494–502.

Note that Muslims, Hindus, and Buddhists are increasingly found living in traditionally "Christian" lands.

DIFFERENCES AFTER TWO CENTURIES

The greatest difference between the world of the Judsons and our world, two hundred years on, is that Christian missionaries are sent out *from* all over the world. It is ironic that the Burmese people the Judsons strived to reach with the gospel two hundred years ago remain unreached today. Yet although Western Christians still engage in reaching them, the Burmese today are more likely to encounter Christ from Filipinos, South Asians, Chinese, or even Brazilians or Nigerians than they are from British or American missionaries. Nonetheless, it should be noted that if Karen Christians in Burma decide to reach out to their (ethnically) Burmese countrymen, even they would be performing the work of cross-cultural missionaries, not of local evangelists. This is important not only with respect to who is doing the witnessing, but in what it signifies: the gospel is not Western in origins or characteristics.[22]

In the past two hundred years, Americans have experienced a rise and fall of their global influence. In 1812 the British Empire was on the rise, and many considered the twentieth century the "American Century."[23] But today, a changing balance of power means that Americans engaging the world find themselves on equal footing with missionaries from Africa, Asia, and Latin America. Americans still have a significant role in the world, but that role is played out on a stage of many characters with their own valuable voices and perspectives.[24] Ironically, this assemblage is more representative of global Christianity than any single ethnic group, Western or non-Western.

The Judsons had trouble identifying the religion of the first Asian they encountered overseas. In this sense, not much has changed. A recent Pew survey shows that Americans still understand very little about other

22. See Lamin Sanneh, *Whose Religion is Christianity? The Gospel Beyond the West* (Grand Rapids: Eerdmans, 2003), in which Sanneh examines the non-Western characteristics of Christianity.

23. Henry Luce, the son of missionaries, urged the United States to break free of isolationism and perform its "missionary" role in the world. See Luce, "The American Century," *Life*, February 17, 1941.

24. See Fareed Zakaria, *The Post-American World* (New York: W. W. Norton, 2008).

religions.[25] Evangelicals, in particular, score poorly compared to atheists and Jews. In 2012, however, one is far more likely than the people of 1812 to encounter someone of another faith, no matter where one lives. That a substantial Burmese community—including the Overseas Burmese Christian Fellowship, who participated in the bicentennial celebration—resides in New England today is but one piece of evidence illustrating this worldwide diversity.

One more difference is that inspiration and activism for "missions" sometimes comes from unlikely sources. Sea captains and their memoirs of yore have been replaced by, among others, courageous journalists. One who tirelessly keeps a vigil on behalf of the poor and the oppressed is Nicholas Kristof. Day after day he presents a case for the poor and oppressed through his *New York Times* editorials and through occasional books such as *Half the Sky*, which he coauthored with his wife, Sheryl WuDunn.[26] This should remind us that much of the education and perspective needed for the missionary enterprise will come from outside the Christian community.

CONCLUSION

Two hundred years ago the challenge for American missions was to channel the enthusiasm of eager students to provide a way for them to express their vocation in a colonial world dominated by Europeans. Today, American Christian students still have their vocations, but now they operate in a multi-polar world where they continue to need encouragement and organizational genius. The challenge for missions agencies today is to adapt to these changing times while retaining the core values of commitment to the Scriptures, to evangelism, and to alleviating human need that have made them successful for the past two centuries. In doing so, the task of world evangelization will be more collaborative (across denominations, ethnicities, and languages), more integrated (vocationally and holistically), and more informed (religiously and culturally). Yet, in the end, it is likely true that were the Judsons alive today, they would once again be the first in line to embark on a lifetime of service in Asia.

25. Pew Forum on Religion & Public Life, *U.S. Religious Knowledge Survey*, September 28, 2010.

26. Nicholas D. Kristof and Sheryl WuDunn, *Half the Sky: Turning Oppression into Opportunity for Women Worldwide* (New York: Vintage, 2010).

7

The Open and Hidden Legacy of Adoniram and Ann Judson

A Burmese Christian Woman's Perspective

May May Latt

INTRODUCTION

This chapter will present the legacy of two of the earliest Baptist missionaries from America to Burma, Adoniram and Ann Judson, and their perspectives on Burma and Burmese Buddhism, as evidenced by Adoniram's letters. Christians in Burma praise the Judsons as our religious forebears, who brought Christianity, the Holy Bible, the Burmese–English dictionary, and schools for girls to Burma. These missionary works can be called the "open legacy" of Adoniram and Ann Judson. On the other hand, there is also a legacy that remains largely hidden from Christians living in Burma. Several letters from Adoniram Judson's personal correspondence indicate a negative view of Burmese Buddhism; this view persists among Burmese Christians. This chapter will discuss the open and hidden legacy of Adoniram and Ann Judson from the perspective of a Burmese Christian woman.[1]

1. The information presented in this section is taken from the pamphlet entitled *Program and Biography of Adoniram and Ann Judson* (Rangoon: Myanmar Baptist

THE OPEN LEGACY OF ADONIRAM
AND ANN JUDSON IN BURMA

The missionary efforts of Adoniram and Ann Judson are commemorated by the Burmese church in an annual celebration on the second Sunday of July, which is called Judsons' Day, the date of their arrival in Burma. The following account is taken from a pamphlet published annually by the Myanmar Baptist Convention (MBC), which provides the program and sermon for the worship service that takes place during that celebration. This account is the open legacy that Christians in Burma read annually.

Adoniram and Ann Judson arrived in Rangoon on the night of July 13, 1813. When they entered Rangoon, Adoniram Judson immediately saw the tremendous golden temple of the Buddha, the Shwedagon Pagoda, "one of the wonders of the world."[2] He realized that his mission would be difficult in Burma. Besides the religion of the country (Buddhism), the government of independent Burma was despotic. In one of his personal letters, which was found and published in 1853, Adoniram wrote:

> A mission to Rangoon we had been accustomed to regard with feelings of horror. . . . The prospect of Rangoon as we approached was quite disheartening. I went on shore just at night to take a view of a place and the mission house; but so dark and cheerless and unpromising did all things appear, that the evening of that day, after my return to the ship, we have marked as the most gloomy and distressing that we ever passed. Instead of rejoicing as we ought to have done, in finding a heathen land from which we were not immediately driven away, such were our weaknesses that we felt we had no portion left here below, and found consolation only in looking beyond our pilgrimage which we tried to flatter ourselves would be short, to that peaceful region where the wicked cease from troubling and the weary are at rest.[3]

Shortly after they settled in at the mission house in Rangoon, the Judsons started learning Burmese. After three years learning Burmese and living in

---

Convention, 1998), 103–19 [in Burmese]. This pamphlet is published annually by the Myanmar Baptist Convention for Judson Day, containing a short history of the Judsons' missionary activity in Burma. Judson Day is a celebration of the "open legacy" of the Judsons that occurs yearly on the second Sunday of July.

2. Courtney Anderson, *To the Golden Shore: The Life of Adoniram Judson* (Boston: Little, Brown, 1956), 168.

3. Francis Wayland, *A Memoir of the Life and Labors of the Rev. Adoniram Judson, D.D.* (New York: Phillips, Sampson, 1853), 1:120–21.

Burma, Adoniram Judson published a grammar of the Burmese language in 1816. Subsequently, he began to develop a vision to translate the Bible into Burmese and to write other Christian books in Burmese. Adoniram completed his translation of the New Testament on July 12, 1823, in his tenth year of living in Rangoon. He completed his translation of the Old Testament on January 31, 1834. He then began work on an English–Burmese dictionary, the first half of which he completed on January 24, 1837.

While living in Rangoon, Adoniram Judson built a wayside chapel, called a *zayat* in Burmese, on the way to the east entrance of the Shwedagon Pagoda. The *zayat*—which he built in the Burmese style, to blend into the Burmese culture—was meant to host people who stopped there for a rest on their way to the pagoda. He took a chance to hold discussions about "who God is, who Christ is, what Christianity is, and what the differences are between Christianity and our indigenous religion."[4] He spread the gospel of salvation, advocating belief in Jesus Christ, the Son of God. In Adoniram's view, salvation in Christianity is not based on one's own effort or practices; rather it is a gift from God based on belief in Jesus Christ. He criticized Buddhism for being a religion that does not offer salvation and is based on personal practices and effort. In the sixth year of his hard work, Adoniram received the first Christian convert, Maung Nau, from among the Burmese people. He baptized Maung Nau on June 27, 1819. After Maung Nau's conversion, Adoniram envisioned building up a church of a hundred converted Christians. After receiving eighteen additional converts in Rangoon in 1823, the Judsons left to Ava (Burmese *Inn-wa*) to begin their mission there.

Since Ann Judson was a schoolteacher, her goal was to start a school for children. Right after they settled in Ava in 1824, she realized her goal, enrolling three native girls. In the same year, war broke out between the British government and the Burmese. Adoniram was accused of being a spy for the British government. He was imprisoned and tortured in Ava. Transferred from one prison to another, his imprisonment lasted twenty-one months. During that time, Ann took care of the family and followed her husband from prison to prison. She bribed prison officials to save the lives of her husband and other foreigners. Due to the stress of carrying all these burdens by herself, Ann Judson died on October 24, 1826 in Amherst (Kyaikkami), but the news of her death arrived in Ava on November 24, 1826.

Although her main mission focused on educating females, Ann was also associated with her husband's translation work. She translated the

4. *Program*, 110.

books of Daniel and Jonah. She believed that her mission to educate females would result in protecting girls from becoming slaves or servants, which was common in Burma in the nineteenth century. Her mission has remained remarkable not only in Burma, but also in the history of American Baptist missions. Sending women missionaries across the world, from the late nineteenth century until the mid-twentieth century, has improved the social status of women. Through the influence of Ann Judson's school, the first female convert, Mah Men-la, opened a village school for boys and girls, so that boys did not need to go to monastic schools to get instruction from the Buddhist priests. Monastic schools provided a monastery education only for boys, but not for girls.

Adoniram and Ann Judson lived ten years in Rangoon and two years in Ava. From Ava, Adoniram moved to Moulmein in 1827 and lived there for twenty-three years among the Karen. At the time of his death, baptized Christians numbered over seven thousand, including one hundred sixty-two ministers, pastors, and assistants, in seventy-four churches throughout the country. Adoniram Judson died at sea on April 12, 1850.

The Judsons are significant as the first American Baptist missionaries in Burma. Annually on Judsons' Day, Burmese Christians remind ourselves about what the Judsons left with us: the Burmese Bible, the English–Burmese dictionary, their sufferings during their mission work in order to spread the Christian gospel among Burmese Buddhists, and their hardship in achieving their first priority of winning coverts, the first of whom was Maung Nau.[5]

The desire to win converts, the main concern of the missionaries, remains a legacy of the Judsons' mission. Before entering the second millennium, Christians in Burma sang a song, saying, "Christ is for Myanmar. Each and every one in Myanmar will believe in Christ. Each Christian has to outreach every citizen of Myanmar to become a Christian in the year 2000."[6] This song was composed in remembrance of Adoniram and Ann

---

5. See Helen G. Trager, *Burma through Alien Eyes: Missionary Views of the Burmese in the Nineteenth Century* (New York: Praeger, 1966), 25. Dana L. Robert also states that "converting people to salvation in Christ was the top priority for both male and female missionaries. . . . Despite Ann Judson's belief that schools were the key to the elevation of women in Burma, school was definitely a secondary strategy for the early Baptist missionary women in Burma." Robert, *American Women in Mission: A Social History of Their Thought and Practice* (Macon, Georgia: Mercer University Press, 1996), 56.

6. The song, entitled "Christ is for Myanmar" (which in Burmese is *Myanmar Pyi Ahtwat Chri-taw*), is composed by Saw Joe Jo.

Judson's mission work in Burma and has become a vision statement of the MBC. In July 2013, the bicentennial of the Christian mission in Burma will be celebrated. After two hundred years of Christianity in Burma, is conversion still our dominant concern as Burmese Christians? What is our attitude toward Burmese Buddhists and Buddhism?

THE HIDDEN LEGACY OF ADONIRAM AND ANN JUDSON

As there is an open legacy of Adoniram and Ann Judson's mission work in Burma, there is also a hidden legacy of the Judsons. The hidden legacy includes how Christians in Burma perceive and relate to Burmese Buddhists. The works of three Burmese scholars may be taken as examples to illuminate the mentality of Christians toward Burmese Buddhists and Buddhism: U Hla Bu (1958), Pe Maung Tin (1961) and La Seng Dingrin (2009).

Since the majority of people in Burma are Buddhists, "Buddhism is an integral part of social and national life."[7] Buddhism in Burma contains many animistic elements. The words "Burma" and "Burman/Burmese" are used synonymously with "Buddhist."[8] Therefore, the country Burma is known as "Burma-Buddhist country" (in Burmese, *Myanmar Buddha bartha naing ngan*). From a Burmese viewpoint, it is often thought that the culture is inseparable from the religion of Buddhism. Hence, when Burmese Christians encounter Buddhism, we often view ourselves as being at odds with our culture, social life, and nationalism. U Hla Bu suggests two attitudes that Christians could have in relating to practitioners of non-Christian religions in Burma:

> [The first attitude is that] we need to have a real understanding and appreciation of the non-Christian living faiths. Before we can evaluate them we should ask ourselves how far we have sufficiently recognized an authentic and cultural core of Buddhism. . . . [The second attitude is that] we need to discover ways and means of conversation and communication in our encounter with the non-Christians. . . . We have to express our faith and practice in forms not alien but indigenous to our culture.[9]

---

7. U Hla Bu, "The Christian Encounter with Buddhism in Burma," *The International Review of Mission* 47, no. 186 (April 1958) 172.

8. Ibid.

9. Ibid., 176–77.

According to the open legacy, the Judsons reached the second attitude addressed by U Hla Bu. The Judsons learned the Burmese language to have conversations, wore Burmese dress to communicate with people, and erected a *zayat* (the wayside chapel) in the Burmese style to host people on their way to the Shwedagon pagoda. However, the Judsons lacked the first attitude, appreciation of the non-Christian living faiths. In his letter on February 20, 1819, Adoniram stated:

> Can *this* darkness be removed? Can *these* dry bones live? On thee,
> Jesus, all our hopes depend. In thee all power is vested, even power to
> make sinful creatures instrumental in enlightening the heathen.[10]

Adoniram Judson, our Christian forefather, believed Buddhism to be a dark religion, and Buddhists the dry bones. He learned Burmese and *Pali* from a Buddhist monk, but this does not mean that he learned, discerned, and acknowledged Buddhism sufficiently. This legacy of the Judsons is not generally known in Burma; however, this hidden legacy highlights the nineteenth-century colonial mentality that the Judsons brought to their Burmese mission.

Professor Pe Maung Tin praised the Judsons for producing the Judson Bible and the Judson Burmese–English dictionary. Although we have so many new versions of the Bible in this era, the Judsons' translation of the Bible is our first and greatest. In fact, the Judsons' use of the Burmese language in the Bible is remarkable in that, according to Tin, "the Judson Bible approached nearer the style of Burmese Buddhist writings, so that it was found to be more readable by the Buddhist monks unacquainted with English."[11] For a century and a half, Judson's successors had worked fantastically in Christian endeavors. Tin mentions that Christian mission works were enormously spread out within this period in Burma: Judson College, Brayton Case, the American Baptist Mission Press, and the Burma Surgeon all stand as evidence of Baptist mission work in the fields of education, agriculture, business, and social service. They established Christian schools, including Burma Divinity School in Insein, and trained doctors and nurses.[12]

The Christian mission had grown rapidly in Burma after 1926 because the Burmese had lost the war to the British. When Burma became a

---

10. Edward Judson, *The Life of Adoniram Judson* (New York: Anson D. F. Randolph, 1883), 123.

11. Pe Maung Tin, "Certain Factors in the Buddhist-Christian Encounter," *South East Asia Journal of Theology* 3, no. 2 (October 1961) 27.

12. Ibid., 28.

British colony, Christianity, the religion of the foreign mission, flourished under favorable conditions. After Burma regained independence in 1948, Christian missionary activities came to an end. Christians believed that U Nu, the Prime Minister, wanted to establish Buddhism as the national religion in Burma. This kind of proposal, however, was nothing new; a similar proposal had been made when the first Burmese kingdom was established in Pagan. Nonetheless, all the institutions founded by missionaries were nationalized after independence. For example, Judson College, founded in 1920, was closed down by the Burmese authorities. Tin asserts that this event was a wake-up call for Christianity, the religion of the West. He says that Judson College was closed down because it would be an American Mission College as long as the memory of Judson was held in respect.[13] Christianity is viewed as a Western religion and Burmese Christians as a Westernized people. While Tin expresses his appreciation of the Judson Bible and the institutions founded by missionaries, he blames the successors of the Judsons—the Christian preachers who neglected Buddhism, its language, *Pali,* and Buddhist monks—for the closing of the College.[14] In his letter on January 18, 1820, Adoniram wrote:

> Here, then, Ah-rah-han, the first Buddhist apostle of Burma, under the patronage of King Anan-ra-tha-men-zan, disseminated the doctrines of atheism, and taught his disciples to pant after annihilation, as the supreme good. Some of the ruins before our eyes were probably the remains of pagodas designed by himself. We looked back on the centuries of darkness that are past. We looked forward, and Christian hope would fain brighten the prospect. Perhaps we stand on the dividing line of the empires of darkness and light. O Shade of Ah-rah-han, weep over thy falling fanes; retire from the scenes of thy past greatness.... The churches of Jesus will soon supplant these idolatrous monuments, and the chanting of the devotees of Buddha will die away before the Christian hymn of praise.[15]

Given the history of Burma where Buddhism has been rooted since the sixth century BC, Christianity perhaps had the best opportunity to thrive during the time of British colonialism in the Burma-Buddhist country. Adoniram learned *Pali* and translated the Holy Bible into Burmese by using some *Pali* and Sanskrit, so that people could read it easily; on the other hand, he also

---

13. Ibid., 30.
14. Ibid., 27–33.
15. Judson, *Life*, 150.

left an exclusivist perspective toward Burmese Buddhism, calling it atheism and its pagodas idolatrous monuments. This hidden legacy of exclusivism and colonialism has been passed down to the Christians in Burma generation after generation. Once attention is drawn to this legacy, we will have a better chance to create peaceful conversation with non-Christians—not only Buddhists but also Hindus, Muslims, and Jews.

An independent Kachin scholar, La Seng Dingrin, has written that "Adoniram Judson has left a conflicting, twofold legacy . . . [Judson's] simultaneous rejection of Burmese Buddhism and his recognition of its indispensability."[16] Dingrin argues that "[the Judsons] had evangelized Burma in a vacuum and hence had no cross-cultural experience." From the perspective of the open legacy, "Judson did not have any problem with Burmese Buddhism and its world view . . . [and] the discussions of his perspective on the religion are unimportant or unfruitful for mission's studies."[17]

Accusing Adoniram of not having cross-cultural experience is questionable, because in the early nineteenth century, it was difficult to have cross-cultural experiences of Asian countries (especially southeastern Asian countries) due to the long travel times by boat. However, Dingrin is correct that Adoniram had a consistently negative view of Burmese Buddhism and rejected it, and then "attempted to replace it with Christianity."[18] The open legacy claims that the Judsons did not seem to have problems with Burmese Buddhism, but the hidden legacy says otherwise. After Adoniram had built the wayside chapel (*zayat*), he wrote in the letter dated February 20, 1819:

> And should this *zayat* prove to be a Christian meeting-house, the first erected in this land of atheists, for the worship of God—a house where Burmans, who now deny the very existence of Deity, shall assemble to adore the majesty of heaven, and to sing with hearts of devotion the praises of the incarnate Saviour.[19]

Dingrin argues that Adoniram described Burmese Buddhism as "atheistic, false, fictitious, idolatrous, and offering no escape," and that he rejected Burmese Buddhism consistently throughout his life in Burma, though he did borrow many terms of *Pali*, the language of Buddhism, and Christianize

16. La Seng Dingrin, "The Conflicting Legacy of Adoniram Judson: Appropriating and Polemicizing against Burmese Buddhism," *Missiology: An International Review* 37, no. 4 (October 2009) 485.

17. Ibid., 486.

18. Ibid., 485.

19. Judson, *Life*, 123.

them, in order to accomplish his mission. Two terms discussed by Dingrin are *bhura*, which is the fundamental Christian term "God," and *kye"ju" to*, which is the Christian term "grace."[20] In his translation, Adoniram used these words, which actually have different attributes in Buddhism. However, by using these words, Burmese Buddhists could easily understand the Christian concept of God and of the merit of the Lord Jesus Christ. Buddhism had provided Christianity with vocabularies and "a worldview in its local appropriation in Burma."[21] Though Adoniram had a negative view of Burmese Buddhism and tried to replace it with Christianity, he affirmed that Buddhism and its language were necessary for his translation work and ministry in Burma. Dingrin concludes that the Judsons have left this two-fold legacy, which made Burma-Buddhist country "the first mission field" of the American Baptist mission.

CONCLUSION

While Christians in Burma carry on the Judsons' open legacy of their hard work, their suffering for the Christian mission, their translation works, their opening of schools for girls, and their other missionary achievements, we also should not neglect the hidden legacy of our forebears. The open legacy of the Judsons is itself a legacy of colonialism; it is a legacy that has a "vision of a whole country open to the gospel of Christ."[22] The legacy, as Dingrin is right to point out, seeks to replace Buddhism with Christianity in Burma. Perhaps Judson's rhetoric seems harsher when judged by today's standards; however, missionaries still seek to bring Christianity to other lands, that impulse has not changed. Nevertheless, this does not mean that there cannot be gracious dialogue and interaction, even while acknowledging differences between religions. We are grateful to the Judsons for their open legacy as our Christian forebears and the bringers of a new religion. However, the hidden legacy must be acknowledged so that Christianity can critique itself and not further perpetuate a colonial legacy.

20. Dingrin, "Conflicting," 485–97.

21. Ibid., 485.

22. See Ethel Daniels Hubbard, *Ann of Ava* (New York: Missionary Education Movement of the United States and Canada, 1913), 236.

8

George Liele

American Missions before Adoniram Judson

SOONG-CHAN RAH

IN HIGH SCHOOL, I would pose the following question to my fellow students: "What was the first ironclad ship used in battle?" Some of my classmates would stare blankly off into space. Most of my classmates and even some of my teachers would quickly state the obvious answer: "The Monitor and the Merrimac"—two armored ships deployed during the American Civil War. Nobody offered up the actual answer: the armored turtle ship (*kobuksan*) used by Korea against the Japanese navy in the sixteenth century.

The common response to the question "Who is the first overseas missionary from America?" is Adoniram Judson. His journey to distant shores earned him the title of "America's First Foreign Missionary."[1] While Judson may be the popular answer to the question, the actual answer is George Liele (sometimes spelled "Lisle"), a freed black slave who left the colonies for Jamaica in 1782 and began a ministry of preaching in 1783/84, nearly three full decades before Judson would sail for Burma from Salem, Massachusetts, in 1812, and a full decade before William Carey sailed for India from England.

---

1. See Faith Coxe Bailey, ed., *Adoniram Judson: America's First Foreign Missionary* (Chicago: Moody, 1999).

Part TWO: Adoniram Judson (1788–1850)

About 1750 in Virginia, America's first overseas missionary was born to Liele and Nancy, both slaves belonging to the Sharpe family.[2] (Adoniram Judson was born nearly thirty-eight years later, in 1788.) George Liele's master, Henry Sharpe, served as a Baptist deacon who eventually settled in the colony of Georgia. George Liele was the child of a Christian father and a slave to a Christian master. Despite the modern incongruity of a Christian slave owner, Sharpe was a church deacon whose slaves actively served in their Baptist Church.

George Liele's conversion occurred in 1773 under the preaching of Rev. Matthew Moore. The white pastor baptized Liele and received him into membership in his church. Liele soon launched into his preaching career, expressing a particular concern for his fellow slaves. George Liele's career, therefore, began as an evangelist and a church planter in the American colonies. Like many Baptist pastors of that time, Liele received no formal training as a pastor. Instead he received approval for his license to preach from his church and a group of white Baptist pastors.

By 1774, Liele had extended his preaching ministry across the Savannah River into South Carolina, gathering slaves together for worship. These gatherings can claim to be the first black church in America. Liele's ministry expanded further into South Carolina with the establishment of a church in Silver Bluff, South Carolina. Liele would be fully ordained into Christian ministry in 1775 and would serve the church until the start of the Revolutionary War. During the Revolutionary War, Henry Sharpe, who served as an officer in the British army, granted Liele his freedom. With his newly granted freedom, Liele began to minister to escaped slaves at Tybee Island, a British stronghold. After the war, Sharpe's children disputed Liele's freedom and had him imprisoned. Faced with limited options, Liele became an indentured servant to a British officer and left the newly formed United States for Kingston, Jamaica, with other evacuating British forces.

George Liele arrived in the mission field of Jamaica when the island colony served as the main center of the slave trade. Four hundred thousand of the six hundred thousand slaves that had arrived in Jamaica had already been shipped to other parts of the Caribbean and North America. Liele was not the first Christian to arrive in Jamaica. Two Roman Catholic priests accompanied Columbus, and the first Moravian missionaries arrived from Europe in 1754. Liele's significance is stated by Clement Gayle

---

2. It seems George took his father's first name as his last name, since slaves did not have their own surnames, only their masters'.

in his biography: "Liele was a pioneer in the sense that he was not just the first Baptist, or the first black minister to preach in Jamaica, but the first one to win a significant number of slaves on the Island to Christ, and certainly, as in the case of the United States, the first to organize a church made up predominantly of negroes on the Island."[3]

In 1783, having arrived as an indentured servant to a Colonel Kirkland, Liele's first priority was to earn his freedom so as to be able to preach throughout the island. Liele himself writes:

> I was landed at Kingston, and by the colonel's recommendation to General Campbell, the governor of the Island, I was employed by him two years, and on leaving the Island, he gave me a written certificate from under his own hand of my good behavior. As soon as I had settled Col. Kirkland's demand on me, I had a certificate of my freedom from the vestry and governor, according to the act of this Island both for myself and my family. Governor Campbell left the Island.[4]

Once free, Liele devoted himself to supporting his family (Liele and his wife had four children) and preaching the gospel message. Liele supported himself through various means, including farming and leasing his horses and carriage for public service. As an expression of his Baptist ordination from the former colonies, Liele continued to preach in private homes and public settings (including services at the Kingston Race Course), drawing crowds of slaves to his gatherings. In a letter written in 1791, Liele reports five hundred converts and four hundred baptisms.[5] In 1789, Liele's congregation had organized to begin work on a house of worship. The church building would be completed in 1793 and become known as the Winward Road Chapel, the first Baptist church on the island.

Liele succeeded in these evangelistic and church planting efforts despite opposition from a powerful constituency on the island. White masters feared the impact upon the slave population if the slaves were to embrace Christianity. Concern arose that "if their minds are considerably enlightened by religion, or otherwise, that it would be attended with the most dangerous consequences."[6] Methodists in Jamaica had not sought the per-

---

3. Gayle, *George Liele: Pioneer Missionary to Jamaica* (Kingston: Jamaica Baptist Union, 1982), 3.

4. Ibid., 13.

5. Ibid., 15.

6. Edward A. Holmes, "George Liele: Negro Slavery's Prophet of Deliverance," *Baptist*

mission of masters to evangelize to the slaves. Liele, on the other hand, took additional precautions not to antagonize the slave owners. He writes, "We receive none in to the church without a few lines from their owners of their good behaviour toward them, and religion."[7] Liele explained that their church bell was not used to summon members to worship, but "to (give notice to) the owners of slaves that are in our society, that they may know the hour at which we meet, and be satisfied that their servants return in due time."[8] Liele also implemented the public reading of a church covenant that outlined the importance of living in accordance to the law.

Despite Liele's numerous efforts to appease the slave owners, he still faced stiff opposition. In one instance "he was charged with sedition after preaching a sermon on Romans 10:1 in which he expressed a strong desire for freedom from sin and its consequences."[9] Trumped up and unjust charges led to Liele being jailed on multiple occasions, such as the following account relates:

> Mr. Liele was charged with preaching sedition, for which he was thrown into prison, loaded with irons, and his feet fastened in the stocks. Not even his wife or children were permitted to see him. At length he was tried for his life; but no evil could be proved against him, and he was honourably acquitted. [However, he was thereupon] thrown into [jail] for a balance due to the builder of his chapel. He refused to take the benefit of the insolvent Debtor's Act, and remained in prison until he had fully paid all that was due.[10]

Despite numerous obstacles, Liele was able to baptize new converts as well as plant and organize new churches. His evangelistic and church planting efforts led to the establishment of the Baptist denomination on the island, with slaves, freedmen, and whites joining churches started by Liele. While Liele had established numerous churches by the end of the eighteenth century, Adoniram Judson was still a child in the Boston area.

In 1802, however, the Jamaican Legislature passed an act restricting preaching to the slaves. "Any person, not duly qualified according to the

---

Quarterly 20 (October 1964) 345.

7. Ibid., 346.

8. Ibid., 347.

9. Gayle, *George Liele*, 17.

10. John Clarke, *The Voice of Jubilee: A Narrative of the Baptist Mission, Jamaica, from Its Commencement; With Biographical Notices of Its Fathers and Founders* (London: J. Snow, 1865), 32.

laws of the island, who should presume to preach or teach in any assembly or meeting of negroes or people of colour, was declared a rogue and vagabond, and ordered to be treated as such."[11] The 1802 Act was annulled by the British Parliament in 1804 but was replaced by an 1805 act that forbade all preaching to slaves. Enforcement of the law resulted in the following gruesome example:

> Some slave owners determined to stamp out a slave prayer meeting. They armed themselves and raided the meeting, with the intention of killing all present. The leader of that group of Christians, Moses Hall, was absent, and his place for that day was filled by his assistant, David. David was seized and murdered. His head was cut off, and those white savages paraded with it through the village as a warning to his followers not to attend Prayer Meeting. In the middle of the village David's head was hung on a pole.[12]

The ministry of George Liele in Jamaica was effectively curbed by the enforcement of these legislative acts. "Liele quietly accepted the restrictions brought on by the restrictive laws and spent his time clearing off the debts owing on his buildings. There is no further account of his activities after the passing of the laws."[13] Eventually, Baptist missionaries would arrive from the United Kingdom. When the British missionaries arrived, close to eight thousand Christians would await them, a result of the ministry of George Liele. While the impact of Liele's ministry continues to this day, Liele himself is buried in an unmarked grave in Jamaica.

George Liele's story reveals an example of hidden and untold stories in American Christianity. Despite preceding Adoniram Judson by three decades, the story of George Liele remains largely unknown. Why does Liele remain unsung as the first American overseas missionary?

There may be a bias against the manner in which Liele left for the mission field. The account of Adoniram Judson departing for foreign shores with the American church supporting his endeavors evokes a romanticized notion of the Western missionary traversing oceans for the sake of the gospel. Judson (and William Carey) have defined our assumptions about the traditional missionary. Crossing cultures and national boundaries to pursue sanctioned missionary work served as the defining characteristic of the Western missionary for the last few centuries.

11. Gayle, *George Liele*, 30.

12. Ibid, 31.

13. Ibid, 32.

Liele, however, left under questionable circumstances. He had sided with the British during the American Revolution. Even though he had been unjustly jailed, going to Jamaica helped Liele escape future imprisonment at the whim of Sharpe's children. There seems to be the absence of a missionary call narrative for George Liele. Knowing Liele's full story, however, reveals the depth of devotion required of him. Liele's call to ministry is clearly revealed in his evangelistic work in the American colonies. As his biographer Clement Gayle notes: "By the time he arrived in Jamaica he was an experienced evangelist and pastor. It is almost impossible to conceive of Liele, the ordained, experienced, Baptist minister seeing himself other than in the role of a missionary to his people."[14] Liele traversed national and cultural boundaries to share the gospel. His ministry in Jamaica endured numerous challenges, including imprisonment. His life clearly reveals a deep missionary calling by God.

Ultimately, I believe that one of the reasons that George Liele's story has not been embraced is because it is a story outside of the traditional parameters of thinking about missions. Liele's story does not have the romantic missionary allure of Adoniram Judson's story. Judson's story provides a more attractive and familiar narrative for the people group more traditionally identified as missionaries. Throughout history, people tend to privilege their own point of view. There are minimal consequences to not knowing another's history.

The winds of change, however, are evident in Christianity. The gentle breeze that whisked away Western culture missionaries to distant shores has returned as the tornado of global Christianity. Christianity is now truly a global faith. Not only is Christianity a global faith, it is a multiethnic and multicultural faith. In the past several decades, we have identified the emergence of a next evangelicalism in the United States.[15] This expression of Christianity encompasses a wider range of ethnicities and cultures than ever before. Christianity is multiethnic and multicultural not only in its global expression but in its American expression, as well.

The next evangelicalism, however, is not merely a recent phenomenon. Ethnic minorities in the United States have long contributed to the spiritual vitality and pioneering work of ministry in this nation. George Liele presents an early example of a vibrant faith outside of the dominant

---

14. Ibid, 14.

15. See Soong-Chan Rah, *The Next Evangelicalism: Releasing the Church from Western Cultural Captivity* (Downers Grove, IL: InterVarsity, 2009).

cultural expression of Christianity in America. Subsequent developments, such as the large number of conversions of freed slaves in the Mississippi delta following the Civil War, the Azusa Street Revival (the birthplace of Pentecostalism, sparked by an African American pastor, William Seymour), and the spectacular growth of Korean-American churches in the decades of the 1970s and 1980s all reflect a vibrancy of the next evangelicalism throughout American history.

Perhaps stories of faith will no longer arise exclusively from a traditional Western narrative. A mistaken notion would be to view the history of non-white Christians as simply branches grafted onto the trunk of traditional Western Christianity. Instead, the various tributaries that comprise the roaring river of global Christianity must be seen as having vital importance. Church history must embrace the rich heritage of cultures and people that now make up the new majority of global Christianity and American evangelicalism.[16] In this scenario, George Liele becomes as significant a figure in the history of American pioneer missions as Adoniram Judson.

16. For more information, see Philip Jenkins, *The Next Christendom: The Coming of Global Christianity* (Oxford: Oxford University Press, 2002); Lamin O. Sanneh and Joel A. Carpenter, eds., *The Changing Face of Christianity: Africa, the West, and the World* (New York: Oxford University Press, 2005); Dana L. Robert, *Christian Mission: How Christianity Became a World Religion* (Chichester, UK: Wiley-Blackwell, 2009); and Rah, *Next Evangelicalism.*

PART THREE

Two Great Mission Pioneers

9

"We Are Confirmed Baptists"

The Judsons and Their Meeting with the Serampore Trio

MICHAEL A. G. HAYKIN

THE EMBRACE OF BAPTIST principles by Adoniram and Ann Judson in 1812 is one of the key turning points in the history of the Baptists in America: it marked this community's *entrée* into the modern missionary movement, an event sealed two years later by the formation of the Triennial Convention. Yet, it was a surprising turn of events, and not least for the principal characters involved, namely, the Judsons and the so-called Serampore Trio: William Carey, Joshua Marshman (1768–1837) and William Ward (1769–1823).

"THE IDEA OF MEETING THE BAPTISTS"

Ann Judson summed up so well what transpired during that significant year of 1812 in a letter that she wrote to a friend in America. The day before, September 6, she and her husband had been baptized by William Ward in the Lall Bazar Chapel in Calcutta.

> You may, perhaps, think this change very sudden, as I have said nothing of it before; but, my dear girl, this alteration hath not

been the work of an hour, a day, or a month. The subject has been maturely, candidly, and, I hope, prayerfully examined for months. An examination of the subject of baptism commenced on board the *Caravan*.[1] As Mr. Judson was continuing the translation of the New Testament, which he began in America, he had many doubts respecting the meaning of the word *baptize*. This, with the idea of meeting the Baptists at Serampore, when he would wish to defend his own sentiments induced a more thorough examination of the foundation of the Pedobaptist system. The more he examined, the more his doubts increased; and, unwilling as he was to admit it, he was afraid the Baptists were right and he wrong. After we arrived at Calcutta, his attention was turned from this subject to the concerns of the mission, and the difficulties with Government. But as his mind was still uneasy, he again renewed the subject. I felt afraid he would become a Baptist, and frequently urged the unhappy consequences if he should. But he said his duty compelled him to satisfy his own mind, and embrace those sentiments which appeared most concordant with Scripture. I always took the Pedobaptist side in reasoning with him, even after I was as doubtful of the truth of their system as he. We left Serampore to reside in Calcutta a week or two, before the arrival of our brethren[2]; and as we had nothing in particular to occupy our attention, we confined it exclusively to this subject. We procured the best authors on both sides, compared them with the Scriptures, examined and re-examined the sentiments of Baptists and Pedobaptists, and were finally compelled, from a conviction of truth, to embrace those of the former. Thus, my dear Nancy, we are confirmed Baptists, not because we wished to be, but because truth compelled us to be. We have endeavored to count the cost, and be prepared for the many severe trials resulting from this change of sentiment. We anticipate the loss of reputation, and of the affection and esteem of many of our American friends. . . . We feel that we are alone in the world, with no real friend but each other, no one on whom we can depend but God.[3]

1. The ship on which the Judsons, along with their fellow missionaries Samuel (1785–1821) and Harriet (1793–1812) Newell sailed to India.

2. A reference to Luther Rice (1783–1836) and the other Congregationalist missionaries, Gordon Hall (1784–1826), Samuel (1787–1869), and Roxana Nott, who had been commissioned with the Judsons. Luther Rice and the three others arrived on August 10. See William H. Brackney, *Dispensations of Providence: The Journal and Selected Letters of Luther Rice* (Rochester, NY: American Baptist Historical Society, 1984), 68.

3. Ann Judson to a friend, 7 September 1812, in Edward Judson, *Life of Adoniram Judson* (New York: Anson D. F. Randolph, 1883), 38–40.

Adoniram had begun working on an English translation of the Greek New Testament while he was still at Andover Theological Seminary from 1808 to 1810 and, among other grammatical and linguistic issues, had found himself perplexed on how to translate the Greek word *baptizō*. Going to India, he also anticipated having to meet Carey, Marshman, and Ward, three convinced Baptists, and having to give a response to any questions they might pose to him about the proper subjects of Christian baptism.[4] The four-month voyage to India from February 19 to June 17, 1812, provided an ideal context in which both he and his wife could intensely study this subject afresh.

On the *Caravan* the Judsons would have primarily had the Scriptures to examine. When they got to India, they were able to consult a variety of Paedobaptist and Credobaptist works over a two-month period.[5] As Ann told her parents the following year:

> After we removed to Calcutta, he [Adoniram] found in the library in our chamber many books on both sides, which he determined to read candidly and prayerfully, and to hold fast, or embrace the truth, however mortifying, however great the sacrifice. I now commenced reading on the subject, with all my prejudices on the Pedobaptist side. We had with us Dr. Worcester's, Dr. Austin's, Peter Edwards's and other Pedobaptist writings. But after closely examining the subject for several weeks, we were constrained to acknowledge that the truth appeared to lie on the Baptists' side.[6]

Here Ann mentions three specific Paedobaptist authors.

---

4. In actuality, the Serampore brethren appear to have made it a matter of principle never to raise this issue with Paedobaptist guests. See Francis Wayland, *A Memoir of the Life and Labors of the Rev. Adoniram Judson, D.D.* (Boston: Phillips, Sampson, 1853), 1:95. See also Carey's account of Judson's thoughts about meeting Carey and his co-workers: Carey to John Williams, 20 October, 1812, cited in Leighton Williams and Mornay Williams, eds., *Serampore Letters: Being the Unpublished Correspondence of William Carey and Others with John Williams 1800–1816* (New York: Putnam's Sons, 1892), 144.

5. See Adoniram Judson, *Christian Baptism* (Calcutta, 1813). It bears noting that the Judsons did not speak to any of the Serampore Trio about this matter until they had reached a decision to become Baptists. For the letter, written on August 27, in which they informed Carey, Marshman, and Ward of their desire to be baptized, see Edward Steane Wenger, comp., *The Story of the Lall Bazar Baptist Church Calcutta: Being the History of Carey's Church from 24th April 1800 to the Present Day* (Calcutta: Edinburgh Press, 1908), 98.

6. Ann Judson to her parents, 14 February 1813, in Edward Judson, *Life*, 40.

Samuel Worcester (1770–1821) was a Massachusetts Congregationalist and an ardent advocate of the theology known as the New Divinity. This theological system was promoted by the heirs of Jonathan Edwards (1703–1758) and combined a fresh approach to issues like the sovereignty of God and the freedom of the will with a careful attention to practical Christianity and the nature of revival. In time, this confluence of theological emphases came to provide a firm foundation for cross-cultural missions. Adoniram's own father, Adoniram Judson Sr. (1752–1826), was also an exponent of this theological perspective, having been mentored by Edwards's confidant Joseph Bellamy (1719–1790). Now, Worcester was the author of two works that dealt specifically with paedobaptism: *Two Discourses on the Perpetuity and Provision of God's Gracious Covenant with Abraham and His Seed* (1805) and *Serious and Candid Letters to the Rev. Thomas Baldwin, D.D. on his book, entitled "The Baptism of Believers Only, and the Particular Communion of the Baptist Churches, Explained and Vindicated"* (1807).[7] Adoniram Judson quotes from both of these works in his *Christian Baptism*,[8] which originated as a sermon three weeks after his baptism and sums up in a public document the fruit of the Judsons' research into the nature of baptism.[9] Reading Worcester's work would have brought back sweet memories of the man, for it was in Worcester's Tabernacle Church in Salem that Judson and his fellow missionaries were ordained and commissioned for their mission to the Far East.[10]

The second author mentioned by Ann was Samuel Austin (1760–1830), among whose works was *A View of the Economy of the Church of God, as It Existed Primitively, under the Abrahamic Dispensation and the*

---

7. Both of these works were published in Salem, Massachusetts, by Haven Pool. The *Two Discourses* were revised for a second edition that appeared in 1807, together with the letters to Baldwin. For Worcester's life, see the biography by his son, Samuel Melanchthon Worcester, *The Life and Labors of Rev. Samuel Worcester, D.D.*, 2 vols (Boston: Crocker and Brewster, 1852). For a brief sketch, see David W. Kling, "Worcester, Samuel," in *The Blackwell Dictionary of Evangelical Biography, 1730–1860*, ed. Donald M. Lewis (Oxford, UK: Blackwell, 1995), 2:1219.

8. See Judson, *Christian Baptism*, 6n, 14n, 15n, 33n, 38n, 42n, 57n, 82n.

9. This sermon was first preached in Calcutta on September 27. Carey judged it to be "a very excellent discourse" (Carey to John Williams, 20 October 1812, in Williams and Williams, *Serampore Letters*, 144) and "the best sermon upon Baptism, that I ever heard" (Carey to William Staughton, 20 October 1812, in James D. Knowles, *Memoir of Mrs. Ann H. Judson:*, 2nd ed. [London: Wightman and Cramp, 1829], 66).

10. See Courtney Anderson, *To the Golden Shore: The Life of Adoniram Judson* (Boston: Little, Brown, 1956), 103–14.

Sinai Law (1807), which Adoniram also refers to in his *Christian Baptism*.[11] Like Worcester, Austin is to be counted among the New Divinity men. He had very close connections with two of the leading theologians of this school of thought: he had studied under Jonathan Edwards Jr. (1745–1801) and later married Jerusha Hopkins, the daughter of one of the leading Edwardseans of the day, Samuel Hopkins (1721–1803).[12]

The third author, Peter Edwards, was an Englishman who had been a Baptist prior to coming to Paedobaptist convictions. He had subsequently written *Candid Reasons for Renouncing the Principles of Anti-Paedobaptism* (1795), a work that went through a number of editions on both sides of the Atlantic.

In the above quotation, Ann does not mention any Baptist authors. Her husband's *Christian Baptism* does indicate explicitly that the Judsons found much food for thought in Abraham Booth's (1734–1806) *Paedobaptism Examined* (1784/1787).[13] Peter Edwards's book noted above was written as a direct response to this work by Booth. Other Baptist figures cited by Judson in his sermon include Henry Danvers (ca. 1622–1687), whose *A Treatise of Baptism* (1673) is primarily a defense of believer's baptism,[14] John Gill (1697–1771), the doyen of Baptist theologians in the eighteenth century and one who was especially critical of the baptism of infants,[15] and

11. See Judson, *Christian Baptism*, 62n.

12. For a sketch of Austin's life, see William B. Sprague, *Annals of the American Pulpit; Congregationalists* (New York: Robert Carter and Brothers, 1857), 2:221–28.

13. See Judson, *Christian Baptism*, 3. Luther Rice also profited by reading Brackney, *Dispensations of Providence*, 73. See the discussion of this book by Sharon James, "Abraham Booth's Defence of Believer's Baptism by Immersion: A Summary," in Michael A.G. Haykin and Victoria J. Haykin, eds., *"The First Counsellor of Our Denomination": Studies on the Life and Ministry of Abraham Booth (1734–1806)* (Springfield, Missouri: Particular Baptist Press, 2011), 132–62. Abraham Booth was described by Andrew Fuller, one who knew him well, as "the first counsellor of our denomination," that is, the English Baptists. Cited in Ernest Payne, "Abraham Booth, 1734–1806," *The Baptist Quarterly*, 26 (1975–1976) 28.

14. See Judson, *Christian Baptism*, 76–77n, where reference is made to *A Treatise of Baptism*. For two studies of Danvers's life and career, see G. Eric Lane, *Henry Danvers: Contender for Religious Liberty* (Dunstable, UK: Fauconberg, 1972) and Richard L. Greaves, *Saints and Rebels: Seven Nonconformists in Stuart England* (Macon, GA: Mercer University Press, 1985), 157–77.

15. See Judson, *Christian Baptism*, 70n, 76–77n. The standard biographical sketch of Gill is John Rippon, *A Brief Memoir of the Life and Writings of the late Rev. John Gill, D.D.* (Harrisonburg, VA: Gano, 1992). For more recent studies of Gill and his theology, see George M. Ella, *John Gill and the Cause of God and Truth* (Eggleston, UK: Go, 1995);

the Seventh-day Baptist Joseph Stennett I (1663–1713), who was one of the most prominent Dissenters of his day.[16]

As Adoniram and Ann studied all of these works and compared what they read with the Scriptures, "truth compelled" them, as Ann puts it, to acknowledge that the better Scriptural arguments lay with the Baptists. It is very evident from both of Ann's letters that Adoniram and Ann began this study as firmly entrenched Paedobaptists. It was only with the greatest of reluctance that they were led to new convictions. In her diary for that summer of 1812, Ann recorded her prayers for the Holy Spirit of God to direct her search. "If ever I sought to know the truth," she wrote, "if ever I looked up to the Father of lights; if ever I gave up myself to the inspired word, I have done so during this investigation."[17]

In the first letter cited above, Ann is also very aware of some of the consequences entailed by their change in sentiments: it will result in the loss of support, financial and even prayerful, of their Congregationalist friends in New England. And it would also mean identification with a body of churches, the Baptists, that were regarded with great disdain by New England Congregationalists. As Adoniram's early Baptist biographer Francis Wayland (1796–1865) noted, in the first couple of decades of the nineteenth century, there was "a strong feeling of sectarian antagonism between the Congregationalists and Baptists."[18] The Judsons, however, were determined to follow biblical truth wherever it led and whatever the cost.

Michael A. G. Haykin, ed., *The Life and Thought of John Gill (1697–1771): A Tercentennial Appreciation* (Leiden: Brill, 1997); and Timothy George and David S. Dockery, eds., *Theologians of the Baptist Tradition* (Nashville: Broadman & Holman, 2001), 11–33.

16. See Judson, Christian Baptism, 77n and 79n, both of which cite Stennett, *An Answer to Mr. David Russen's Entitul'd Fundamentals without a Foundation; or, a True Picture of the Anabaptists* (London: D. Brown, S. Crouch, and J. Baker, 1704). For the life and ministry of Stennett, see especially "Some Account of the Life of the Reverend and Learned Mr. Joseph Stennett," in *The Works of the Late Reverend and Learned Mr. Joseph Stennett* (London, 1732), 1:3–36; R. L. Greaves, "Stennett, Joseph (1663–1713)," in Greaves and Robert Zaller, eds., *Biographical Dictionary of British Radicals in the Seventeenth Century* (Brighton, Sussex: Harvester, 1984), 3:205–6; Allen Harrington and Martha Stennett Harrington, "The Stennetts of England," online: http://www.blue-hare.com/stennett/tpgindex.htm#prefixa.

17. Cited by Sharon James, *My Heart in His Hands: Ann Judson of Burma; A Life, with Selections from Her Memoir and Letters* (Darlington, UK: Evangelical, 1998), 55.

18. Wayland, *Memiors*, 1:86. For Adoniram Judson's statement that he would now be regarded by his Congregationalist friends as "a weak, despicable Baptist," see Worchester, *Life and Labors*, 1:102.

Adoniram described such determination at the close of *Christian Baptism* as he pled with his hearers (and later readers):

> My brethren, diligently use the means of discovering the truth. Put yourselves in the way of evidence. Indulge free examination. Though the sun shines with perfect clearness, you will never see that light which others enjoy, if you confine yourselves in a cavern, which the beams of the sun cannot penetrate. Be assured, that there is sufficient evidence on this subject, if you seek to discover it. But if your love for truth is not sufficiently strong to make you willing and strive for the discovery of evidence, God will probably leave you to be contented with error . . . therefore, to stimulate your minds to candid and energetic research, prize truth above all things.[19]

"THE RIGHT STAMP FOR MISSIONARY UNDERTAKINGS"

The Judsons' love for the truth endeared them to the Serampore missionaries. This was surely part of what William Carey had in mind when he wrote in October of 1812 to the Welsh Baptist John Williams (1767–1825), then pastoring in New York City, that Adoniram Judson and Luther Rice, who was subsequently baptized, were "men of the right stamp."[20] This phrase seems to have stuck in Carey's mind as an apt description of Adoniram, for four years later he told the American Baptist Thomas Baldwin (1753–1825) that Adoniram was "a man of God, one of the right stamp for missionary undertakings."[21] The context of this second use of the phrase "right stamp" sheds important light on Carey's overall view of the Judsons' mission and the Judsons themselves. Carey's remarks obviously stemmed from time that he spent with the Judsons: talking with them, getting to know them well, and praying with them.

---

19. Judson, *Christian Baptism*, 88.

20. Carey to John Williams, 20 October 1812, cited in *Serampore Letters*, ed. Williams and Williams, 145.

21. Carey to Thomas Baldwin, 10 September 1816, cited in "English Baptist Mission," *American Baptist Magazine and Missionary Intelligencer*, 1 (1817–1818) 100. In the paragraph following this remark, Carey observes that Judson is "remarkably self-denying and prudent," two characteristics Carey deemed vital for being a missionary. See also Carey to Thomas Baldwin, 25 July 1816, cited in *American Baptist Magazine and Missionary Intelligencer*, 1 (1817–1818) 64, where he states that Judson is "a good man and truly possesses the spirit of a missionary."

Baldwin had asked Carey about the feasibility of the Judsons' missionary labors in Burma.[22] Carey first of all noted that he and Baldwin, and by implication the Judsons, as well, lived in what had to be regarded as "an eventful period" of world history in which the "gospel has entered nearly every country" in the East. Carey was confident that behind this gospel advance was "the zeal of the Lord of the hosts," probably a reference to Isaiah 9:7, in which God's determination to establish the messianic kingdom is predicted.[23] In this regard then, Carey did not believe "a mission impracticable in any country." The veteran missionary recognized that some mission scenarios posed more problems than others, but eventually all "will assuredly give way to persevering labours."

Carey then looked specifically at Burma. It was a truly difficult situation in a number of ways, something that Carey knew about since his son Felix Carey (1786–1822) had been a missionary there.[24] But if a Burmese mission had not been at all feasible, Carey would never have encouraged Felix to go there in 1808, nor would the Serampore community have "persisted in it so long." Moreover, Carey believed that the Burmese "government is not intolerant in religious things." But when all was said and done, Carey believed that missions was God's great work. As he put it to Baldwin: "Success . . . does not depend on might nor on power, but on the Spirit," a clear reference to Zechariah 4:6, which had long been a favorite text with Carey when he thought about the advance of the kingdom of Christ. For instance, Carey had written in his classic statement of missionary principles, *An Enquiry Into the Obligations of Christians to Use Means for the Conversion of the Heathens*, during the early 1790s:

> However the influence of the Holy Spirit may be set at nought, and run down by many, it will be found upon trial, that all means which we can use, without it, will be ineffectual. If a temple is raised for God in the heathen world, it will "not be by might, nor

22. For what follows, see Carey to Baldwin, 10 September 1816.

23. This phrase also occurs in 2 Kgs 19:31 and Isa 37:32.

24. For a biography of Felix Carey, see Sunil Kumar Chatterjee, *Felix Carey: A Tiger Tamed* (Hooghly, India: Sunil Kumar Chatterjee, 1991). See also D. G. E. Hall, "Felix Carey," *Journal of Religion* 12, no. 4 (October, 1932) 473–92. Hall documents the tumultuous political situation to which William Carey is presumably alluding in "Felix Carey," 477–80. When Felix assumed the post of Burmese ambassador to the British government in Calcutta, his father made the famous remark that his son had "shrivelled from a missionary into an ambassador." Chatterjee, *Felix Carey*, 114. For the remarkable problems associated with Felix being the Burmese ambassador, see Hall, "Felix Carey," 484–91.

by power," nor by the authority of the magistrate, or the eloquence of the orator; "but by my Spirit, saith the Lord of Hosts."[25]

Both here and in the letter to Thomas Baldwin, Zechariah 4:6 was used to express a pneumatological conviction central to the thinking of both Carey and the circle of men who had sent him and the others of the Serampore community to India: without the gracious aid of the Holy Spirit, they could do nothing for God. Now, in the hands of some, such a conviction might have induced a temper of passivity. But not so with Carey and his friends. In them it produced a deep confidence that as they gave themselves whole-heartedly to the work of God, God the Holy Spirit would use their efforts to ultimately advance the reign of Christ.[26]

A CONCLUDING WORD

When the Judsons eventually arrived in the Burmese kingdom in July of 1813, Felix Carey and his wife were an immense help in getting the American missionaries settled in Rangoon.[27] In the months that followed, Felix was thrilled to have Adoniram and Ann as missionary coworkers. As he wrote to his father a number of months later about the Judsons, "They are just cut out for the [Burmese] Mission," an echo of his father's statement about Judson being of "the right stamp." As Felix continued, "Mr. Judson has a splendid grasp of the [Burmese] language and is the very colleague I wanted."[28] The missionary partnership between the Judsons and Felix Carey and his wife was not to last. In June of 1816, Carey, Marshman, and Ward told Thomas Baldwin and the other members of the mission board of the Triennial Convention that Felix had "gone into the service of his Burman majesty."[29] More bluntly, and more famously, the elder Carey told his close friend John Ryland Jr. (1753–1825) back in England that his son had "shrivelled from a missionary into an ambassador."[30]

25. See, e.g., William Carey, *An Enquiry into the Obligations of Christians to Use Means for the Conversion of the Heathens* (Leicester, UK: Ann Ireland, 1792), 78–79.

26. This is well expressed by Carey et al. to US Baptist Board of Missions, 25 June 1816, cited in "English Baptist Mission," *American Baptist Magazine and Missionary Intelligencer* 1 (1817–1818) 186–87.

27. Hall, "Felix Carey," 481.

28. Cited by S. Pearce Carey, *William Carey*, 8th ed. (London: Carey Press, 1934), 320.

29. Carey et al. to US Baptist Board of Missions, 25 June 1816.

30. Cited by Chatterjee, *Felix Carey*, 114. For the remarkable problems surrounding

But Carey and his son were right about Judson and his wife. As the history of the American Baptist mission to Burma unfolded, it became quite obvious that this couple were indeed of the "right stamp." It was a stamp that bore the deep impress of the Spirit of Jesus, and Adoniram unwittingly described himself and Ann when he told Luther Rice what sort of missionaries the Burmese Baptist mission needed:

> Humble, quiet, persevering men; men of sound, sterling talents (though perhaps not brilliant), of decent accomplishments, and some natural aptitude to acquire a language; men of an amiable, yielding temper, willing to take the lowest place, to be the least of all, and the servant of all; men who enjoy much closet religion, who live near God, and are willing to suffer all things for Christ's sake, without being proud of it—these are the men.[31]

Felix being the Burmese ambassador, see Hall, "Felix Carey," 484–91.

31. Judson to Luther Rice, 14 November 1816, cited in *American Baptist Magazine and Missionary Intelligencer* 1 (1817–1818) 185.

10

Bloodlines and Bloodletting
Historic Themes in Baptist Missions

Jeff Iorg

Two Baptists were shipwrecked on a deserted island. They were there for many months before their rescuers arrived. After the celebratory hugs and handshakes, one of the rescuers observed a beautiful building made of carefully stacked stones on a ridge overlooking a bay. He asked, "What's that building on the hill?"

One of the Baptists answered, "That's First Baptist Church. We built it as soon as we arrived so we could have a place to worship God and to invite anyone who might live on the island to join us and hear the gospel." Then another rescuer saw another building in the valley just down the hill. It had a similar shape, but was made of driftwood and not quite as nicely constructed. He asked, "Well, then what's the building in the valley?"
"Oh," replied the other castaway, "That's Second Baptist."

Baptists are a missional people, which is an admirable quality. Some-times, however, our missionary convictions and efforts result in conflict among us. These two aspects of Baptist identity are often closely connected. At least since events surrounding William Carey in 1792, being on mission is in our Baptist blood, an inextricable part of our identity. We can no more deny that heritage than a man can deny he has his father's receding hairline or a woman has her mother's beautiful eyes.

My premise in this chapter is this: the characteristics and convictions found among the first Baptist missionaries and missionary organization have become part of our bloodline (who we are), as well as a source of occasional bloodletting among us. Baptists are at their best when they live out their bloodline—missions—and at their worst when their missional convictions produce conflict—bloodletting—over issues related to that mission.

Our missionary forefathers, focusing primarily in this chapter on William Carey, made sure (to use two modern phrases) being "on mission" is "in our DNA." It is part and parcel of who we are. Because of their emerging missionary convictions, early Baptists experienced conflicts that have been replicated and repeated through the generations, until, in some cases, they have become part of the character—or caricature—of Baptist identity. Those early experiences are the seedbed from which modern Baptist missions practices have emerged, both to our credit and detriment.

This chapter will focus on examples of this reality in three areas: doctrinal concerns, strategic structures, and deployment of missionary personnel. It will draw primarily on the early experiences of and events associated with William Carey, and will include corresponding contemporary examples from my part of the Baptist family, the Southern Baptist Convention.

DOCTRINAL CONCERNS

John Ryland Sr., a prominent English Baptist pastor, was leading a ministerial meeting in Northampton in 1792. He asked his colleagues to suggest a topic for discussion. William Carey proposed for consideration "the duty of Christians to attempt the spread of the gospel among heathen nations." Ryland Sr. replied, "Young man, sit down. When God pleases to convert the heathen, He will do it without your aid or mine!"[1]

This infamous exchange seems harsh to most modern Baptists, a stunning rebuke to a question most Baptists would consider stimulating discussion fodder. What theological milieu would prompt such a reply, and make this proposal so controversial as to offend such an esteemed minister? Eighteenth-century Baptists in England were generally divided into two groups: General Baptists (Arminian) and Particular Baptists (Calvinist).

---

1. Timothy George, *Faithful Witness: The Life and Mission of William Carey* (Birmingham, AL: New Hope, 1991), 53.

General Baptists had drifted from orthodoxy on many theological issues, such as the deity of Christ. By the time of Carey, they were largely irrelevant in Baptist leadership or evangelical Christianity.[2]

Particular Baptists, on the other hand, with their adherence to the London Confessions (1644, 1677, and 1689) had initially retained their passion for the gospel and commitment to biblical fidelity. By the eighteenth century, however, Ryland Sr.'s attitude reflected a "hardened attitude in Baptist thinking,"[3] which took Calvinism to an extreme, denying any human agency in conversion, and its corollary, any human responsibility to preach the gospel among the unconverted. While that perspective may not have been shared by all, it was the predominant view among many leading Particular Baptist pastors. This was the theological background to the rebuke Carey received from Ryland Sr.[4]

Andrew Fuller, in his tract *The Gospel Worthy of All Acceptation*, was one of the most prominent critics of this "hardened attitude." Fuller based his conclusions on careful study of the Bible's many admonitions for the lost to repent and be converted, his reading of the lives of John Eliot and David Brainerd, who preached aggressively and passionately to the unconverted, and his discovery of Jonathan Edwards's *Inquiry into the Freedom of the Will* (1754). These influences came together to produce a more balanced theological position, advocating the Supremacy of God in salvation, but also requiring appropriate expressions of human responsibility.

Carey came under Fuller's influence through reading his tract *The Gospel Worthy of All Acceptation* (1785). These theological adjustments to the position advocated through hyper-Calvinism stoked the missionary embers already burning in Carey. If Fuller's assertions were accurate, the offshoot of this theological position was clear for Carey: for the unconverted to hear the gospel, someone had to deliver the message to them. Hence, he proposed to the ministerial association the discussion about taking the gospel to the heathen, and in doing so crystallized the theological debate related to the question of missionary responsibility.

Baptists throughout history have affirmed the totality of God's supremacy in salvation, while also acknowledging human responsibilities like repentance and faith.[5] Baptists have spent four centuries arguing these

2. Ibid.

3. Ibid.

4. Ibid.

5. See Adrian Rogers, ed., *The Baptist Faith and Message* (Nashville: LifeWay, 2000).

points and continue to do so. The Southern Baptist Convention is currently experiencing another such debate among theologians of various stripes.[6] Baptists seem to enjoy this kind of debate, evidenced by the large crowd that assembled to hear Dr. R. Albert Mohler and Dr. Paige Patterson when they debated these issues at the SBC Pastors' Conference in 2006. Fortunately, for the sake of unity and to the disappointment of some in attendance, the debate was more of a spirited discussion among friends than the free-for-all some had anticipated.[7]

For Baptists, theology matters a great deal. Theology matters because its implications determine our mission. Theology is worth debating because the stakes are high. Most Baptists, no matter their place on the divine sovereignty–human responsibility spectrum, take the Bible seriously when it describes the eternal state of the unconverted. Correctly appropriating the doctrine of salvation and its corollary of missional responsibility are important because we believe the eternal destiny of people is at stake. Being a Baptist is a convictional decision to align with missional theology and practice. When Adoniram Judson decided to become a Baptist while en route to India, it was more than a decision about the subject and mode of baptism, it was a commitment to biblical fidelity and the missionary task.

For some, there is significance in debating the question "which comes first—theology or mission?" Most Baptists would in theory claim theology precedes mission. Belief informs behavior, at least on a theoretical level. But in the ebb and flow of kingdom life, theology and mission are more intertwined than sequenced. The former may inspire the latter, but the latter then shapes the former. Our theology drives us to the mission field, but theology is then tested, shaped, and adjusted by what is encountered on the mission field. This is seen among contemporary missionaries, for example, in the debate about contextualization. The crucial question is how much theological adaptation is possible, and in what areas of faith and life is it possible, before sound theology is compromised. Theology drives mission, but mission shapes theology (or at least demands its reconsideration and culturally appropriate affirmation in every context).

This is not an easy process. It was probably not easy for Carey to raise mission-related questions when he knew a theological debate would ensue.

6. See, e.g., Brad J. Waggoner and E. Ray Clendenen, *Calvinism: A Southern Baptist Dialogue* (Nashville: B & H Academic, 2008) and Kenneth Keathley, *Salvation and Sovereignty: A Molinist Approach* (Nashville: B & H Academic, 2010).

7. Michael Foust, "Patterson, Mohler: Calvinism Shouldn't Divide SBC," *Baptist Press*, June 13, 2006, online: http://www.bpnews.net/bpnews.asp?id=23457.

Questioning theological convictions of people in power is a surefire means of creating conflict. Beginning with Carey and continuing to the present, Baptists have been willing to confront theological systems undermining their sense of missional responsibility. They have also been willing to raise the alarm when theological drift has threatened the mission they cherish. For example, in the previous generation, Southern Baptists had a prolonged and often bitter struggle to reclaim biblical fidelity.[8] Now, in this generation, we are in the midst of reforming missionary strategies and structures.[9] One is insufficient without the other. Reforming one naturally leads to reconsideration of the other.

Sound theology and missionary responsibility are both our heritage as Baptists. Holding to both simultaneously, with whatever tension that produces, is also our heritage. It is in our blood to strive for theological integrity and missional effectiveness. Trying to maintain both is also the cause of some bloodletting in almost every generation.

STRATEGIC STRUCTURES

Baptists are independent-minded people who are not reticent to form or reform organizations to suit their particular missionary passion. The first Baptist missionary organization formed in 1792 as a result of Carey's preaching and passion. After preaching his famous "expect great things, attempt great things" message at an associational meeting, he feared the meeting would adjourn with no resulting action. He pleaded with the moderator, Andrew Fuller, "Oh, sir, is nothing to be done? Is nothing again to be done?" His emotional plea turned the tide and the association adopted a resolution calling for the creation of the Baptist Missionary Society.[10]

The Society was modeled after trading companies popular at the time with individual donors contributing varying amounts for a common purpose. This pattern was replicated by other early mission societies among other Christian groups. The Baptists, however, led the way in creating

8. See, e.g., Paul Pressler, *A Hill on Which to Die: One Southern Baptist's Journey* (Nashville: Broadman & Holman, 1999) and Jerry Sutton, *The Baptist Reformation: The Conservative Resurgence in the Southern Baptist Convention* (Nashville: Broadman & Holman, 2000).

9 See, e.g., Chuck Lawless and Adam W. Greenway, eds., *The Great Commission Resurgence: Fulfilling God's Mandate in Our Time* (Nashville: B & H, 2010).

10. H. Leon McBeth, *The Baptist Heritage: Four Centuries of Baptist Witness* (Nashville: Broadman, 1987), 185.

missionary-sending and missionary-supporting organizations. The societal method of missionary support was thus inaugurated.[11]

While this development might seem rather benign to modern Baptists, it was an entrepreneurial innovation in its day. Carey's famous tract, *An Enquiry into the Obligations of Christians to Use Means for the Conversion of the Heathens*,[12] contains within the title this explosive idea: to use means. While modern commentators often focus on "obligation" and "conversion," the call "to use means" may have been the most breathtaking new idea in the pamphlet. Carey called for a new extra-biblical ecclesiastical structure—a society—to establish policies, commission missionaries, and provide their financial support.[13] While councils, committees, societies, and mission boards are too numerous today to count, most Christians who read Carey's pamphlet or heard him speak had never conceived of an organization with global missional responsibility.[14] Most eighteenth-century believers never traveled any significant distance from their homes and had little concept of Christian organization beyond their local churches or associations. The proposal of the creation of a society for combining the missionary efforts of many believers and churches was a remarkable innovation.

Yet, in this innovation—necessary in its time—there is also the seed of much dissension, conflict, and confusion for Baptists. Once missionary responsibility was delegated by the local church to another institution or organization, the potential for each congregation's global missional responsibility to be diminished was also introduced. Baptist churches in the late 1700s were not committed to or organized enough to advance global missions. Carey's call for a society to network the individuals and churches who supported such an effort was commendable, and probably necessary to break through the theological opposition and spiritual lethargy limiting such a movement at that time. The creation of such a society (and thousands more—about 4,410 existed worldwide in 2006[15]) has sometimes served the unintended purpose of separating global missional responsibil-

11. See David W. Bebbington, *Baptists through the Centuries: A History of a Global People* (Waco, TX: Baylor University Press, 2010), 218.

12. Published Leicester, UK: Ann Ireland, 1972.

13. Andrew F. Walls, *The Missionary Movement in Christian History: Studies in the Transmissions of Faith* (Maryknoll, NY: Orbis, 1996), 244.

14. Ibid., 246.

15. David B. Barrett, et al., eds., "Missiometrics 2006: Goals, Resources, Doctrines of the 250 Christian World Committees," *International Bulletin of Missionary Research* 30, no. 1 (2006) 27–30.

ity from congregational life. The role of Baptist believers and their churches has been reduced to praying for and paying for others to do missionary work. Occasionally, one of these believers, perhaps inspired by the work of a favored society, might join the missionary force. That was often the only way a local congregation invested personnel in global missionary work. Gradually, the global mission responsibility shifted from the local church to societies supported by select believers or endorsed by congregations, associations, or conventions.

Some Baptists, Southern Baptists in particular, have advocated an associational or convention model for organizing missionary endeavors. Contrast is often drawn in these denominations between "societal" and "associational" approaches, usually with some disdain expressed for societal methods. In practical terms, however, denominational mission boards function as privately-owned mission societies. They are often organized or structured just like independent societies with one caveat. They serve only one client: their specific denominational brand of Baptists. The "pray and pay" expectations are the same, just within one denominational family rather than as a broader Christian movement.

In recent years, the International Mission Board of the Southern Baptist Convention has attempted to reinvent itself into a vehicle for local church missionary involvement, rather than a substitute for it.[16] This change has been driven by theological convictions about the responsibility of local congregations to fulfill the Great Commission, enhancement of travel and communication strategies, which make widespread missionary activity more possible, the financial challenges of supporting a fully-funded missionary force, and accommodating the current generation's proclivity for direct involvement in smaller projects rather than supporting large organizations on a grand scale.

Some leaders today advocate for direct local church mission programs devoid of any outside society or denominational mission board. While the churches in Carey's day "whether episcopal, or presbyterian, or congregational could not effectively operate overseas missions,"[17] churches today, particularly in North America, have both the resources and will to do so. Technological and travel advances have made it possible to send many short-term mission teams, as well as establish and maintain international partnerships. Information about mission history and strategy are widely

16. See *International Mission Board*, online: http://www.imb.org/main/default.asp.
17. Walls, *Missionary Movement*, 246.

available, enabling churches to more readily craft their own strategy.[18] One study showed more than half of North American churches with a weekly attendance over two thousand maintain their own mission-sending organization.[19] This model is also being widely implemented in smaller churches, even advocated for in very small churches.[20]

The means Carey initiated for global outreach, the mission society, is a core strategy for Baptists around the world. Much good has come from using this method, but perhaps at the expense of keeping all believers in local churches lashed to the burden of global mission responsibility. The proliferation of mission societies on every continent, in almost every country and for every conceivable purpose, has diversified missionary outreach. It has also, perhaps to the detriment of Baptist churches, diluted efforts by expending so much money on administration, promotion, fundraising, and management of thousands of well-meaning organizations, rather than investing more resources directly in the field. Baptist mission societies are part of our bloodline and the source of some bloodletting from time to time. They are, and will remain, a mixed blessing among us.

PERSONNEL DECISIONS AND CHALLENGES

The core of every cross-cultural mission program is the missionary, the person sent from one culture to another to communicate the gospel. Most missionaries, starting with Carey, advocate and prioritize using indigenous leaders to sustain their work. But, in the beginning, Carey, his family, and his associates were pioneer missionaries, serving where there were no indigenous leaders. They are, in that regard, models for missionaries today who are engaging what are commonly called "unreached people groups" in very challenging spiritual environments.

Many of the personnel issues that surfaced in the early missionary's first few years of service are still crucial issues for today's missionary candidates. These issues are not so much sources of conflict between Baptist

18. See Craig Ott et al., *Encountering Theology of Mission: Biblical Foundations, Historical Developments, and Contemporary Issues* (Grand Rapids: Baker Academic, 2010), 206–7.

19. Robert J. Priest et al., "U.S. Megachurches and New Patterns of Global Mission," *International Bulletin of Missionary Research* 34, no. 2 (2010) 97–104.

20. See "Churches on Mission," *International Mission Board*, online: http://www.imb.org/main/lead/default.asp.

groups but are, instead, sources of interpersonal tension within our decisions about deploying people for missionary service. As a seminary President and trainer of new missionaries, I have observed two issues that arise from modern-day missionary selection processes that mirror the story of the conflicts among the first Baptist missionaries.

First, some people who are passionate for missionary service are simply not suited for the task. The first missionary appointed by the Baptist Mission Society was not Carey, it was Dr. John Thomas (1757–1801). Thomas was a Baptist physician from England who had spent many years in Bengal, India, and wanted to return. He did so, under the auspices of the Society, but to the detriment of the Carey family who accompanied him. Dr. Thomas was apparently a well-meaning, sincere Christian with little business sense and even less of a concept of sacrificial identification with his mission or those he was sent to reach. His poor fiscal management and lifestyle choices cost the Carey's dearly as they scrambled to overcome Thomas's poor decisions that led to financial hardship for all of them.[21]

There was another person in the initial traveling party also not truly suited for the assignment, at least not in the way or at the time she joined the effort. William Carey's wife, Dorothy, was not supportive of her husband's passion for global ministry. She had never previously traveled more than ten miles from her birthplace and flatly refused to accompany him to India. He took their oldest child, Felix, and prepared for departure. The ship's sailing was delayed. Carey used the opportunity to rush home and implore Dorothy to go with him. She changed her mind, packed herself and four children, and bade farewell to her family—all within a few hours.

She regretted her decision almost from the time the ship departed. Dorothy did not adjust to missionary life; the climate challenges, cultural adaptations, grinding poverty, strange sicknesses, and the death of a child took their toll. After about three years, she lapsed into a deep depression. She lived her final thirteen years in a padded room behind a locked door.[22]

With regard to Thomas, it is easy to understand why the Society would select him as a missionary candidate. He was well-educated and honorably employed as a physician. He had experience in the country where he was to be deployed. He gave evidence of Christian commitment and reported a call to missionary service. By many measurements, he seemed like a strong candidate for missionary appointment.

21. George, *Faithful Witness*, 97.
22. McBeth, *Baptist Heritage*, 186.

Giving the embryonic nature of the effort, it is not surprising the concept of formal "assessment" was not part of deciding who the Society would send as their first missionaries. Today, seminaries who train candidates and societies or denominations that send missionaries are much more thorough in assessing the qualities that candidates must have to serve effectively. This sometimes creates tension when fellow Christians—often passionate and sincere—must be told they are not suitable and will not be appointed, sent, or supported. This is a painful process for missionary candidates, mission administrators, and those who educate people toward fulfillment of a global mission.

The sad story of Dorothy Carey has many themes that could be explored. Modern critics, however, must remember the context when considering the actions of both Carey and the Society. It would seem, however, even accounting for the cultural differences from that day to this that a spouse's willingness to serve, overall health, and family responsibilities should have been given more credence in the decision-making process. There were early missionary couples with remarkably different stories. Adoniram and Ann Judson, for example, had a long and fruitful ministry and marriage while serving in trying missionary circumstances. Many early missionary wives served with distinction and several, including Ann, gave their lives for the expansion of the gospel. Judson later married Sarah Boardman, the widow of one of his missionary partners. They worked together for many years, while having eight children, and were also a model of a healthy missionary marriage partnership.

Candidate assessment today includes careful consideration of family relationships and health concerns in determining who will be sent as an international missionary. It is painful to deny appointment to a person because they are not physically or emotionally healthy enough to withstand the rigors of missionary service. It is even more painful, and often creates additional relational pain, to deny a person appointment because their spouse or child is not prepared for the challenges of being a missionary. The issues of call, sacrifice, and destiny are often interwoven with confusion, frustration, and anger in sorting out these issues. In cultures with more hierarchical family structures, these issues are sometimes exacerbated (resulting in even greater conflict) or minimized (masked by denial, leading to worse problems in the long run). Nevertheless, the sad story of Dorothy Carey underscores the significance of considering family and health dynamics in the context of determining God's call to a missionary assignment and God's timing related to missionary service.

The second significant personnel issue emerging from these early examples is that missionaries work best in pairs, partnerships, and community. Carey's work changed significantly for the better in 1799 when the Serampore Trio formed. William Carey, Joshua Marshman, and William Ward created a community around the Serampore Covenant. The resulting synergy—personal and professional—propelled the mission to its greatest work in the following decades. This development has been called a "major novelty" and unique contribution of the first Baptist missionaries. It was a major novelty because the development of this integrated community confounded both the cultural and theological backgrounds of its participants. It was a unique development, an unusual social structure, and a model for future missionaries working in community.[23]

The first missionaries, Thomas and Carey, went together to the field, but not as a true partnership or team. Their relationship endured but it cannot be cited as a model. Thomas was too irresponsible and did not share the strategic and personal commitments that made Carey such a remarkable missionary. While the first missionaries probably tried to work in community, it was the later group that accomplished the goal and set the standard for contemporary emulation. Simply assigning people to work together is not an adequate means of creating dynamic missionary communities. Taking the time to build true partnerships and teams is a means to missionary success. Missionaries, facing the myriad challenges of cross-cultural living, work best when they have a partner or team to share the load.

CONCLUSION

The early Baptist missionary efforts are seedbeds for issues that define us and divide us. Our theology and missiology are closely linked. We are passionate about both and willing to endure conflict over doctrine and/or practice to ensure eternal life for as many people as possible.

Our strategies and structures matter, and we enjoy creating and recreating them in a never-ending search for greater impact. We have formed and reformed societies and denominational bodies by the thousands, with no signs of slowing this process, in our zeal to find the most effective and

23. Ralph D. Winter, "William Carey's Major Novelty," *Missiology: An International Review* 22, no. 2 (1994) 207.

efficient ways to accelerate the fulfillment of the Great Commission.[24] Strong opinions on these matters energize our debates, fuel our successes, and sometimes divide and diminish our efforts.

Baptists challenge each other to answer God's call to missionary service, and then evaluate their calling with rubrics based on years of practical experience sending and supporting missionaries. Sometimes, we celebrate God's call by affirming the person and sending them to the mission field with our blessing. Other times, we confound the call by refusing to send Christians we simply do not believe will serve effectively. Missionaries struggle with loneliness, isolation, and depression because of their work environments. Sometimes they do not get along with one another, undermining efforts to create supportive partnerships, communities, and other networks. Baptist missionaries, like all other Baptists, know they need each other but sometimes struggle with relational harmony. These issues were part of the earliest Baptist missionary stories and they are still part of the unfolding story of Baptist missions today.

Baptists are a missionary people. It is in our blood and sometimes puts blood on the rug. What we started in 1792, we have been living out for more than two hundred years. Our missionary zeal is not abating. The tensions that result show no signs of lessening. What a heritage, and what a wild ride the future will be!

---

24. The author has recently concluded a year-long assignment as a member of the Focus 21 Task Force, which was asked to recommend ways "to more effectively and efficiently fulfill the Great Commission" through the California Southern Baptist Convention.

11

The Sacrifices of Dorothy Carey and Ann Judson

Two Sides of the Same Coin

CHRIS CHUN

MANY WORDS HAVE BEEN justly dedicated in honor of these two pioneering men, William Carey and Adoniram Judson, yet their wives, who were pivotal to their ministry, seldom receive the attention they deserve. In the context of this wider volume, this chapter is a small tribute to their first wives, often unsung heroines despite their enormous sacrifices.

Dorothy Carey and Ann Judson in some ways might be polar opposites of each other, yet in other ways, they may be two sides of the same coin. Stark contrasts between them, for those who are familiar with both of their stories, almost seem too obvious. On one hand, nineteenth-century biographers may not have always painted sympathetic portraits of Dorothy, often portraying her as a psychotic, unwitting, illiterate, and reluctant minister's wife who caused an enormous amount of distress and distraction to the frontier missionary work in India. For example, John Brown Meyer wrote, "Mrs. Carey had little sympathy with her husband's tastes, and though her predisposition to mental disease was the occasion of constant anxiety, he ever treated her with noble tenderness."[1] In like manner, C. M. Yonge, another prolific nineteenth-century British novelist, commented:

> It was an unlucky marriage, for [Dorothy] was a dull, ignorant woman, with no feeling for her husband's high aims or superior powers, and the business was not a flourishing one; but he never manifested anything but warm affection and tenderness towards this very uncompanionable person.[2]

On the other hand, Ann Judson was often exalted as a pious exemplar of a missionary wife whose faith under adversity shone, as a heroine who sacrificed her health and eventually her life to save Adoniram through tireless efforts in bringing food and clothes, and also by pleading with guards and government officials to take care of her husband while he was a prisoner of war in Let Ma Yoon, a prison infamous for its cruelty. Compared to Dorothy, Ann was from a noble family. She was a well-educated ministry partner, who along with her husband was instrumental in reaching Burmese women in a cultural context in which women could be reached only by other females. Sharon James describes that while Ann "did not challenge the traditional biblical teaching regarding male leadership," her life "challenges the stereotype of the nineteenth-century Christian female as merely passive, decorative or weak."[3] Dana Robert also underscores the almost legendary, saint-like stature of Ann Judson in nineteenth-century Protestantism, when her name became "a household word in the United States" and "a stock item of female hagiography across denominational lines."[4] How then, can these two radically contrasting historical figures be similar, let alone be spoken of as two sides of the same coin? Before attempting to answer this question, brief biographical sketches of these two remarkable women might be in order.

1. John Brown Myers, *William Carey: The Shoe Maker Who Became "The Father of Modern Missions"* (London: S. W. Partridge, 1887), 19.

2. Charlotte Mary Yonge, *Pioneers and Founders; or, Recent Workers in the Mission Field* (London: Macmillan, 1874), 97.

3. Sharon James, *My Heart in His Hands: Ann Judson of Burma; A Life, with Selections from Her Memoir and Letters* (Durham, UK: Evangelical Press, 1998), 203.

4. Dana L. Robert, "The Mother of Modern Missions," *Christian History and Biography*, Spring 2006, 24. See also Dana L. Robert, *American Women in Mission: A Social History of Their Thought and Practice* (Macon, GA: Mercer University Press, 1997).

DOROTHY PLACKETT CAREY (1756–1807)

On June 10, 1781, a cobbler named William Carey married Miss Dorothy Plackett. When she married him, Dorothy was not a minister's wife by any means. She had instead married a shoemaker in the town of Northampton, England, where production of shoes was renowned. After the marriage, William became a lay preacher (1785) and then a pastor (1789). We do not know how Dorothy personally felt about becoming a pastor's wife; nonetheless, we do know that in following William's ordination, Dorothy reaffirmed her faith through believer's baptism by the hand of her husband and became a Baptist in October 1787.

Dorothy bore six of William's children: Felix (1785–1822), Peter (1789–1794), Jabez (b. 1793), and Jonathan (b. 1796), but William and Lucy died at the age of two in England.[5] Dorothy knew about her husband's zeal for the lost around the world; however, it is uncertain whether she also shared his missionary passions. I suspect probably not. William sensed a strong missionary calling to go to India, but his wife simply refused. Historical speculation is that the effects of several factors contributed to Dorothy's decision not to follow her husband to India. First, she "knew too little," in that she did not have the benefit of education and lacked knowledge about the world and its foreign cultures, as they had been explored by Christopher Columbus and Captain James Cook. Second, she "knew too much," in that she had quite possibly heard all of the contemporary rumors of the East India Company taking a hostile stance toward missionaries in India for meddling with their religious, social, and local customs. These historical variables do have some plausibility. Perhaps the most important reason might have been the fact that Dorothy was five months pregnant when Andrew Fuller and John Ryland Jr. first came to visit her to inquire about missionary possibilities. Her answer: a resounding no. After giving birth, she was reluctant to take a nursing infant to India.[6]

Dorothy's unwavering decision to stay would have surprised many people in the Baptist Missionary Society, since by nineteenth-century standards, it was generally accepted that a wife would follow her husband wherever he would lead her. In light of this predicament, William had to

5. For a helpful chart of Carey's family tree, see Timothy George, *Faithful Witness: The Life and Mission of William Carey*, special movie companion edition (Worcester, PA: Christian History Institute, 1998), xi.

6. See James R. Beck, *Dorothy Carey: The Tragic and Untold Story of Mrs. William Carey* (Grand Rapids: Baker, 1992), 67–83.

adjust his plans. He and his eldest son, Felix, would go to India for a year, and would return to bring the rest of the family. This plan would have given ample time for father and son to settle in India, as well as to provide opportunity to inform Dorothy about the living conditions there; perhaps this time could have been an occasion for Dorothy to share her husband's missionary vision and make it her own calling. This option would have been more palatable, or even sensible, for reluctant Dorothy and her situation. This plan, however, did not happen. As events progressed, pressure mounted at home. Dorothy's dear sister, Kitty Plackett, who did not wish to see the family split and would have been tremendous help in raising her young children, volunteered to join the Careys in this adventure, an enormous psychological consolation, as well as a pivotal factor for Dorothy's eventual concession to follow her husband to India.

Be that as it may, in Debhata, India, Kitty's well-intended, benevolent support later turned out to be a devastating blow for her sister when Kitty fell in love and married Mr. Charles Short, deciding not to accompany Dorothy to Malda, a place where her five-year-old son, Peter, fell ill and eventually died, on October 11, 1794. Due to the financial struggles that the Carey family had to face, Dorothy's new life in India at one point included having to stress over whether her children would eat their next meal and finding housing that was not foul. Still, the death of her son was by far where things really took a turn for the worse for Dorothy. The Hindu taboo against touching corpses and graves must have accentuated this painful experience all the more. Having to dig a grave and bury their beloved son on their own because no Indians would help was surely cause for resentment, not only against Indian superstition, but also against her husband for bringing his family to India. The loneliness she felt in this foreign land was not only qualitatively different from anything she had ever experienced, but became an overwhelming obstacle for Dorothy to handle. Five people would have attended Peter's burial: Dorothy, William, and their three children. Psychohistorian James Beck assesses how this tragic experience might have affected Dorothy's permanent mental health:

> The trauma of Peter's death and burial had temporarily pushed William, the kind and meek shoemaker-turned-missionary, to become a somewhat highhanded colonial baron.... These sad events pushed William to a temporary extreme. But these same events pushed Dorothy to a permanent extremity.[7]

7. Beck, Dorothy Carey, 105–6.

While there is no doubt that the story of Dorothy is "troubling,"[8] even "tragic,"[9] it is often overshadowed by her husband's glorious legacy, whose influential repercussions are still being felt all over the world to this day. Without minimizing William's historic contributions, his wife's story deserves to be told, not as an embarrassing side of William's private life to be quietly ignored, but as one of a woman willing to sacrifice her very life to give birth to the modern missionary movement. Surely, H. Miriam Ross must have had a historical point when she wrote, "Certainly there is more to this woman's story than the dismissive words of her husband's biographers would indicate."[10]

Baptist historian H. Leon McBeth vividly summarizes how Dorothy came to accompany her husband in India, underscoring what I think demonstrates a need for another full-length treatment of this remarkable woman who, for good or for ill, stands at the fountainhead of modern missions:

> Carey accepted appointment as a missionary to India, and the date for sailing was set before Dorothy was even told about it. Carey urged her to go with him, but she at first refused. So Carey took their oldest child, Felix, and set out for the ship. However, the sailing was delayed, and Carey took the opportunity to rush back home and plead once more with Dorothy to join him. With many tears, she yielded and had only a few hours to pack all her possessions for herself and four children, bid farewell to family and friends, and leave England forever. She was scarcely aboard ship when she came to regret her decision, and she adapted poorly in India. The heat and humidity took their toll, and she was subject to severe fevers. Their grinding poverty, the uncertainty of their existence, and the death of one child proved more than she could cope with, and she lapsed into deep and debilitating depression. For the last thirteen years of her life, she lived in a single room, with padded walls, behind a locked door. Somewhere in missionary history a word of compassion should be written for Dorothy Carey, who paid a high price for Baptist missions and never knew why.[11]

8. H. Miriam Ross, "What About Dorothy?" *Evangelical Missions Quarterly* 28 (October 1992) 363.

9. Beck, *Dorothy Carey*, 15.

10. Ross, "What About Dorothy?" 362.

11. H. Leon McBeth, *The Baptist Heritage: Four Centuries of Baptist Witness* (Nashville: Broadman, 1987), 186–87.

Whichever way historians spin it, these are the facts in Dorothy's life, which can only be characterized as sacrifice. Whatever might have been her motive for going to India, she gave up her comfortable and familiar life in England to follow her husband's missionary vision. There, she lost her son and her physical and mental health deteriorated to an incapacitated state, and finally, her anguished experience in the mission field came to an end on December 8, 1807. After her ship sailed to India on that early morning of June 14, 1793, Dorothy Carey, first wife of the "father of modern missions," never once came back to her homeland.

ANN HASSELTINE JUDSON (1789–1826)

Ann Hasseltine's decision to marry Adoniram Judson was none other than an answer to her lifelong missionary dream. From the beginning, Adoniram did not hide this fact when he, rather audaciously, asked John Hasseltine for his daughter's hand in marriage:

> I have now to ask, whether you can consent to part with your daughter early next spring, to see her no more in this world; whether you can consent to her departure to a heathen land, and her subjection to the hardships and sufferings of a missionary life; whether you can consent to her exposure to the dangers of the ocean; to the fatal influence of the southern climate of India; to every kind of want and distress; to degradation, insult, persecution, and perhaps a violent death. Can you consent to all this, for the sake of Him who left His heavenly home, and died for her and for you; for the sake of perishing, immortal souls; for the sake of Zion and the glory of God? Can you consent to all this, in hope of soon meeting your daughter in the world of glory, with a crown of righteousness, brightened by the acclamations of praise which shall resound to her Saviour from heathens saved, through her means, from eternal woe and despair?[12]

This astonishing letter written to a prospective father-in-law, one can only imagine, must have stunned him. When Adoniram proposed to lovely Miss Hasseltine the possibility of taking their courtship to another level, she told him that her father's permission was needed to move forward. Courtney Anderson suggests that Mr. Hasseltine's eyes must have popped nearly out

12. Adoniram Judson, "Extract of Letter to John Hasseltine," in James D. Knowles, *Memoir of Mrs. Ann H. Judson, Wife of the Rev. Adoniram Judson Missionary to Burmah*, 2nd ed. (London: Wightman and Cramp, 1829), 41–42.

of his head when he read the letter![13] Amazingly enough, her parents left their daughter to make up her own mind on this matter. Understandably, Rebecca Hasseltine, Ann's mother, wished her not to leave America; nevertheless, she told her that she would not withhold consent if Ann chose to go. Ann's father supported her with his blessings, whichever path she should take. This goes to show the enormous confidence Ann's parents had in their twenty-two-year-old daughter's capacity to make a permanent and life-altering decision. While it remains uncertain how much of Ann's decision to accept Adoniram's marriage proposal had to do with her love for Adoniram, or to do with fulfilling her burden to serve as a missionary in a foreign land, both factors were significant in her decision to marry him. This story is the polar opposite of how Dorothy Carey decided to marry William and to follow him to India.

Ann married Adoniram on February 5, 1812. Just two weeks later, on February 19, the newlyweds sailed for Calcutta, India. It must have been quite the honeymoon! Both Ann and Adoniram, having been raised in Congregational families, were aware that, upon their arrival, they would be ministering alongside the famous English Baptist missionaries of Serampore, led by, of course, William Carey, Joshua Marshman, and William Ward. As one of the first American missionaries, Adoniram wondered how they could work together with their differences concerning infant baptism. Although all of their first converts would be adults, he wondered if he should also baptize the children of these new believers in a heathen land. To solve these theological and practical issues, the Judsons launched an intense study of Scripture and prayer during their four-month voyage to India. As a result of this endeavor, the Judsons drastically changed their views on baptism. Had they known that the Baptist missionaries of India had a policy to avoid such controversies, they might never have started this investigation. At any rate, in describing her husband, Ann wrote, "the more [Adoniram] examined, the more his doubts increased; and unwilling as he was to admit it, he was afraid the Baptists were right and he wrong." Ann added, "but as his mind was still uneasy he again renewed the subject. I felt afraid he would become a Baptist, and frequently urged the unhappy consequences if he should."[14] Modern readers may not be able to fathom

13. See Anderson, *To the Golden Shore: The Life of Adoniram Judson* (Valley Forge, PA: Judson Press, 1987), 83.

14. Ann Judson, "Letter to a Friend about Becoming a Baptist," in *A Sourcebook for Baptist Heritage*, ed. H. Leon McBeth (Nashville: Broadman, 1990), 208.

these fears associated with being Baptists. Ann, who was also from an aristocratic Congregational family, wrote to her closest friend back home, "Can you, my dear Nancy, still love me, still desire to hear from me, when I tell you I have become a Baptist?"[15] Her apologetic tone captures this difficult dilemma. In spite of Ann's initial denial of the views of credobaptism, she finally came to the same biblical conviction as did her husband. At much personal cost, Ann finally decided to leave her respectable social standing, and much to her shame and pride, she told her friend, "My dear Nancy, we are confirmed Baptists, not because we wished to be, but because truth compelled us to be. . . . We anticipate the loss of reputation, and of the affection and esteem of many of our American friends."[16] Ann and Adoniram Judson essentially left America as Congregationalists, but arrived in India as Baptists. They knew this decision would severely affect their relationships with friends and family back in America. Consequently, the Judsons, in all good conscience, could no longer accept financial support as Congregational missionaries. It was then important for Baptists back home to organize a board to support these new Baptist missionaries, which also became the occasion for the Baptist Mission Board to begin the founding of the Triennial Convention in 1814, which by the way, was the first national Baptist denominational meeting held in the United States. When the Judsons arrived in Calcutta on June 17, 1812, both the Indian government and the East India Company were opposed to missionary activities. Soon thereafter, they were ordered to leave. Even though the Judsons arrived in India first, on July 13, 1813, they were commissioned again as missionaries to Burma, but by the Baptists this time.

The story of how Ann arrived on the mission field might be antithetical to Dorothy's, but Ann, similarly, would undergo a grievous experience of burying her second child, Roger William Judson, in Burma. That said, unlike Dorothy, it appears that an encounter with grief did not overtake her. In fact, Ann's firm grasp of theodicy surfaces in the midst of burying her eight-month-old son under a great mango tree on May 4, 1816:

> All the Burmans who were acquainted with us endeavoured to sympathise with us, and consol us under our loss. Our little Roger was the only legitimate child of foreign parents in the place, consequently he was quite a curiosity to the Burmans. But what shall I say about the improvement we are to make of this heavy

15. Ibid., 207.
16. Ibid., 208.

affliction? We do not feel a disposition to murmur, or to inquire of our Sovereign why he had done this. We wish, rather, to sit down and submissively under the rod and bear the smart, till the end of which the affliction was sent, shall be accomplished.[17]

Ann was more than a pretty face, she was a theologian in her own right. In her early years, Ann received a thorough education in Bradford Academy and was not timid in thinking about weighty theological matters. Her contemporary and most significant biographer, James Knowles, described how she "thirsted for the knowledge of gospel truth, in all its relations and dependencies," and emphasized how she practiced "daily study of the scripture." Ann also drank deeply from the piety of John Bunyan and David Brainerd. Furthermore, she was not intimidated by scholarly minds of her generation and read their work "with deep interests." Among these authors were Joseph Bellamy, Samuel Hopkins, and their mentor, Jonathan Edwards. Knowles fondly recounted his firsthand encounter with Ann when she drafted her theological reflection and finally finished her transcriptions of Edwards's magnum opus, *A History of Work of Redemption*:

> With Edwards on Redemption, she was instructed, quickened, strengthened. Well do I remember the elevated smile which beamed on [Ann's] countenance, when she first spoke to me of its precious content. She had transcribed, with her own hand, Edwards's leading and most striking remarks on this great subject.[18]

With this type of learned background, it is no wonder she was able to produce a catechism in Burmese to instruct the young converts, as well as to engage in translation work with her husband in 1819. About eight years into missionary work, in 1822, Ann became so ill that she needed to return to America for a rest, but she also capitalized on this window of time to write a book, entitled *An Account of the American Baptist Mission to the Burman Empire*. When it was published in 1823, her book immediately became a bestseller and proved to be a significant impetus for missions by way of recruiting churches to support missionary enterprises with their finances and prayers. The legacy of Ann Judson is renowned: "Ann became the model of who was in all senses a partner with her husband;"[19] and as David Bebbington writes, "The couple became missionary icons, inspiring

---

17. Knowles, *Memoir*, 124.

18. Ibid., 20.

19. James, *My Heart*, 202.

the extension of missionary enterprise into Assam, Siam, southern India, China, and Liberia."[20]

When Ann returned to Burma, the Judsons needed to relocate from Rangoon to Ava, but in 1824, a war broke out between the English and Burmese. Out of this political turmoil, all Westerners were immediately suspected of being British spies, and although Adoniram was an American, he was likewise seen as a spy and was put in prison on June 8, 1824. John Piper captures what afflictions Ann had to undergo during her husband's imprisonment:

> Ann was pregnant, but she walked the two miles daily to the palace to plead that Judson was not a spy and that they should have mercy. She got some relief for him so that he could come out into a courtyard. The prisoners got vermin in their hair amid the rotting food and had to be shaved bald. Almost a year later, they were suddenly moved to a more distant village prison, gaunt, with hollow eyes, dressed in rags, crippled from the torture. There the mosquitoes from the rice paddies almost drove them mad on their bloody feet. The daughter, Maria, had been born by now, and Ann was almost as sick and thin as Adoniram, but she still pursued him, with her baby, to take care of him as she could. Her milk dried up, and the jailer had mercy on them and actually let Judson take the baby each evening into the village fettered and beg for women to nurse his baby.[21]

Adoniram was eventually released on November 4, 1825, but the damage was already done. These extended days of sacrificial distresses for the sake of her husband had finally taken a fatal toll on the already frail body of Ann. So eleven months after his release, on October 24, 1826, Ann Hasseltine Judson passed away. Six months later, their baby Maria, who had also endured this ordeal, would die.

TWO SIDES OF THE SAME COIN

How then, could these two radically contrasting historical figures be similar, let alone be spoken of as two sides of same coin? Despite chronological

20. David W. Bebbington, *Baptists through the Centuries: A History of a Global People* (Waco, TX: Baylor University Press, 2010), 220.

21. John Piper, "Adoniram Judson: 'How Few There Are Who Die So Hard'; The Cost of Bringing Christ to Burma," in *Filling Up the Afflictions of Christ: The Cost of Bringing the Gospel to the Nations in the Lives of William Tyndale, Adoniram Judson, and John Paton* (Wheaton, IL: Crossway, 2009), 98–99.

and geographical overlaps, Dorothy and Ann never met, and their differences in psychosocial temperament, as well as sociological background, are miles apart. Nonetheless, they have much in common.

Both Dorothy and Ann were first wives whose husbands married twice again after their passing.[22] Both of their husbands were, and still are, some of the most celebrated pioneers in an epoch known as the great century of missions. Be that as it may, my case for seeing them as two sides of the same coin rests mostly on sacrifices they made, and the manner in which their sacrifices were manifested through two very different individuals, personalities, backgrounds, and circumstances. They both lived at a time when departing from the comforts of Western civilization to the dangers of the ocean and embarking on a mission were thought of as death warrants for Westerners, whether it be from disease (of which both suffered chronically) or the jaws of wild animals. Being on the forefront of what later became the Protestant missionary movement also meant having no clue about what adversity might lie ahead. Although Dorothy's family was from the Anglican tradition in England, and Ann's, the American Congregationalist, they both left their own traditions to follow their husbands' Baptist beliefs, during a time when Baptists were still considered marginalized sects of Christianity.

Needless to say, Ann's sacrificial legacy is well remembered, and deservingly so. The same could not be said of Dorothy, however. It is true that she did not share the same missionary visions with her husband as did Ann, but Dorothy, undoubtedly, gave up much. Beck has rightly asserted, "Perhaps her sacrifice was not a voluntary one, but it was a sacrifice nonetheless."[23] The most painful experiences for these women would have been losing their children in foreign soil, away from family and friends. For

---

22. For short summaries of William Carey's wives, see George, "The Three Mrs. Careys," in *Faithful Witness*, 156–62. After Dorothy's passing on May 9, 1809, William Carey married Charlotte Amelia Rumohr (1761–1821), and in the summer of 1822, he wed once more, to two-time widow Grace Hughes, who cared for him in his illness for the remaining years of William's earthly life. For further reading on Judson's wives, see Arabella Stuart, *The Lives of the Three Mrs. Judsons* (Springfield, MO: Particular Baptist Press, 1999); for a more recent treatment, see Candi Finch, "So That the World May Know: The Legacy of Adoniram Judson's Wives," in *Adoniram Judson: A Bicentennial Appreciation of the Pioneer American Missionary*, ed. Jason Duesing (Nashville: B&H Academic, 2012), 101–25. Like Carey, Judson married two more times following Ann's death. Sarah Boardman (1803–1845), a widow, married Adoniram in 1834. Subsequent to Sarah's passing, Emily Chubbuck (1817–1854), a famous American poet who wrote the biography of Sarah and also collected sources for Francis Wayland's biography of Judson, married Adoniram on June 22, 1846.

23. Beck, *Dorothy Carey*, 14.

Dorothy, it was the loss of her beloved Peter, and for Ann, her baby Roger. Indeed, each of them had faced tremendous obstacles to ministry and endured personal afflictions. This notwithstanding, the two heroines stood by their men, even with broken physical (Ann) and mental (Dorothy) health, and weathered through tough times. Most of all, they gave their own lives to the mission field, all the while never enjoying the fruits of their sacrifice, since they died before their husbands reached the pinnacles of their careers as missionary celebrities. These sacrificial lives, when taken into account together, conjure the image of two sides of one coin.

The phrase "Behind every great man stands a great woman" might be a fitting tribute to Dorothy and Ann, unless, of course, the modern egalitarian reader has qualms with the word "behind." However, whether behind, beside, or in front of, it might suffice to say that these great women were companions to, and laid sacrificial foundations for, the completion of their husbands' historic ministries.

Index[1]

Abayasekera, Annathaia, 68
Account of an Embassy (Symes), 76
Account of the American Baptist Mission (Judson), 133
Ah-rah-han, 90
Akbar the Great, 44
Alexander VI, Pope, 18
Ambedkar, Bhimrao Ramji, 41
American Baptist Mission Press, 89
American Baptist, 63, 71–72, 87, 89, 92, 109, 112
American Civil War, 93, 99
American Mission College, 90
American Revolutionary War, 94, 98
American Society for Foreign Missions, 67, 77
Anabaptists, 18
Anan-ra-tha-men-zan, King, 90
Anderson, Courtney, 75, 130
Andover Newton Theological School, 65–66, 69
Andover Theological Seminary, 65–67, 77, 105
Anglicanism, 7, 11, 71, 135
Appeals to the Christian Public (Roy), 43–57
Appies, Leonardo, 68
Arianism, 12, 17
Austin, Samuel, 105–7

Bagby, William, 72
Baldwin, Thomas, 106, 109–11
Baptism, 17, 56–58, 71–72, 95, 104–9, 116, 127, 131–32
Baptist Missionary Society, 11, 13, 117, 127
Baptist World Alliance, 71
Basu, Rajnarain, 27
Basu, Ram, 33, 35
Bebbington, David, xiii-xiv, 133
Beck, James, 128, 135
Bellamy, Joseph, 106, 133
Bengal Asiatic Society, 23
Bentinck, William, 40
Bible translation, 4, 10–11, 37, 43, 80–81, 86, 89, 92, 104–5, 133
Boardman, Sarah, 122
Booth, Abraham, 107
Bosch, David, 18
Brahmin caste, 11, 28, 34–35, 44
Brahmo Samaj, 45
Brainerd, David, 7–8, 25–26, 115, 133
Brayton Case, 189
Bridges to God (McGavran), 24
British Parliament, 21, 97
Brown University, 65, 76
Brown, David, 7
Bu, U Hla, 88–89
Buddhism, 71, 79, 81–82, 84–92
Bunyan, John, 3, 133
Burma Divinity School, 89
Burma Surgeon, 89
Burnouf, Eugène, 22

1. The co-editors are grateful to Chris Chun's research assistant, Stephen Reynolds, for preparing the index of this book.

Index

Calvinistic Baptists. *See* Particular Baptists

Campbell, Archibald, 95

Candid Reasons (Edwards), 107

Carey, Dorothy Plackett, 32, 35–36, 121–22, 125–32, 135–36

Carey, Edmund, 30–31

Carey, Felix, 32, 110–11, 121, 127–29

Carey, Jabez, 127

Carey, Jonathan, 127

Carey, Lucy, 127

Carey, Peter, 32, 35, 127–28, 136

Caste System, 11, 22, 27–41, 45

Castro, Emilio, 69

Catholicism, 9, 18, 20, 23, 33, 69, 94

Charter Act of 1813, 21

Chaucer, Geoffery, 3

Christian Baptism (Judson), 106–9

Chun, Chris, ix, xviii, 125–36

Church of Scotland, 22

Clifford, John, 6

Coke, Thomas, 7

Colebrooke, Henry Thomas, 22

Columbus, Christopher, 31, 94, 127

Colvin, James, 27

Communism, 79–80

Confucius, 43

Congregationalism, 71, 75, 106–8, 119, 131–32, 135

Cook, James, 127

Costas, Orlando, 63–73

Costas, Rose, 64, 72–73

Cutler, Manasseh, 75

Dalit caste, 27–41

Danvers, Henry, 107

Daoism, 79

Dingrin, La Seng, 88, 91–92

Doyle, Sean, ix, xvii, 42–59

Duff, Alexander, 16, 22

Dussel, Enrique, 69

Dyche, Thomas, 31

East India Company, 7, 33, 44, 127, 132

Edinburgh, Scotland, 11–12, 16, 67–69

Edwards, Jonathan, 7–9, 106, 115, 133

Edwards, Jonathan, Jr., 107

Edwards, Peter, 105, 107

Eliot, John, 26, 115

Enquiry (Carey), 9–10, 13, 20, 25, 33, 110, 118

Erskine, John, 8

Eschatology, 9

Ethnic Realities and the Church (McGavran), 24

Faithful Witness (George), 3, 15, 135

Fort William College, 40, 44

Frederick IV, King, 18

Free University of Amsterdam, 65

Freedom of the Will (Edwards), 115

Friend of India, 43

Friesen, Abraham, 18

Fuller, Andrew, 10–11, 13, 20, 115, 117, 127

Ganges, 40

Garret-Evangelical Theological Seminary, 65

Gayle, Clement, 94, 98

George, Timothy, ix, xvi, 3–15

General Baptists, 11–13, 114–15

Gerhard Oncken, Johann, 25, 72

Gill, John, 107

Gospel Worthy (Fuller), 115

Grant, Charles, 7

Great Awakening, 9

Great Commission, 6–7, 10, 13–14, 16–20, 72, 74, 119, 124

Great Commission Baptist. *See* Southern Baptist Convention (SBC).

Grenfell, George, 72

Half the Sky (Kristof and WuDunn), 83

Hall, Gordon, 64, 67

Hall, Moses, 97

Hall, Robert, 13

Hare, David, 27

Harijans. *See* Dalits

Harvard University, 76

Hasseltine, John, 77–78, 130

Hasseltine, Rebecca, 131

Haykin, Michael, x, xviii, 103–12

Hinduism, 4, 10–11, 22, 29, 36, 39–40, 42–45, 58–59, 79, 81–82, 91, 128

History of Work of Redemption (Edwards), 133
Homer, 10
Hooker, Thomas, 3
Hopkins, Jerusha, 107
Hopkins, Samuel, 107, 133
Humble Attempt (Edwards), 8

Iliad (Homer), 10
Infanticide, 39–41
International Congress on World Evangelization (1974), 24
International Mission Board, 119. *See also* Southern Baptist Convention
InterVarsity, 68
Iorg, Jeff, x, xviii, 113–24
Islam, 9, 29, 35–36, 39, 44, 57–59, 79, 81–82, 91

James, Sharon, 126
Jenkins, Philip, 70
Jesuits, 23
Johnson, Todd, x, xvii, 74–83
Jones, William, 22
Judson, Ann Hasseltine, 38, 72–74, 77–78, 84–88, 103, 105–8, 111–12, 122, 125–26, 130–36
Judson, Maria, 134
Judson, Roger William, 132
Judson Bible, 89–90
Judson College, 89–90

Kali, 33–34, 40
Karen tribe, 80, 82, 87
Kirkland, Colonel, 95
Knowles, James, 133
Kobuksan, 93
Koyama, Kosuke, 68
Kristof, Nicholas, 83
Kron Princess Maria, 7
Kshatriya. *See* Caste.

Latin Vocabulary (Dyche), 31
Latin America Mission (LAM), 70
Latt, May May, x, xvii-xviii, 84–92
Liele, George, 72, 93–99
Life of David Brainerd (Edwards), 7
Life of William Carey (Smith), 3

Livingstone, David, 41
London Confessions, 115
London Missionary Society (LMS), 5, 78
Lutheranism, 18
Macaulay, Thomas Babington, 21
Mangalwadi, Ruth, 38
Manu, 40
Marshman, Hannah, 38
Marshman, Joshua, 27, 38, 42–59, 103, 105, 111, 123, 131
Martyn, Henry, 5, 8
Massachusetts Missionary Society, 77
McBeth, H. Leon, 129
McGavran, Donald, 24
Men-la, Mah, 87
Methodists, 7, 11, 13, 95
Meyer, John Brown, 125
Michaelangelo, 18
Mills, Samuel, 66–67
Missionary Rock, 66–67
Milton, John, 3
Missio Dei, 20
Missiology, 15–26, 65–66, 80, 123
Moe, Cynthia, 64
Mohammed, 43, 55–58
Mohler, R. Albert, 116
Moon, Lottie, 72
Moravians, 4, 7, 26, 94
Mott, John, 67
Munshi, 33, 35
Myanmar Baptist Convention (MBC), 85, 88

Native Americans, 80
Nau, Maung, 86–87
New Divinity School, 106–7
Newell, Samuel, 64, 66–67
Newton, John, 4
Next Christendom (Jenkins), 70, 99
Next Evangelicalism (Rah), 70, 98
Nichols, Clarke, 31
Nicolai, Philipp, 25
Northampton Baptist Association, 5
Nott, Samuel, 64, 66–67
Nottingham, 5, 7, 19
Nu, U, 90

Index

Oduyoye, Mercy, 68

Odyssey (Homer), 10

Old, Thomas, 32

Oussoren, A.H., 34

Overseas Burmese Christian Fellowship, 83

Paedobaptism Examined (Booth), 107

Pal, Krishna, 37

Pali, 89–91

Papal Bull (1493), 18

Particular Baptists, 12–13, 114–15

Patrick, Saint, 7

Patterson, Paige, 116

Phillips Academy, 66–67

Phule, Mahatma Jotiba Govindrao, 41

Pedobaptism, 104–7, 131

Pietà (Michelangelo), 18

Piper, John, 134

Plackett, Kitty, 128

Plan of the Society for the Establishment of Missions among the Heathen (Coke), 7

Plutschau, Henry, 18, 26

Precepts of Jesus: the Guide to Peace and Happiness (Roy), 42–43, 45

Presbyterianism, 11, 119

Proposal for Establishing a Protestant Mission in Bengal and Bihar (Brown and Grant), 7

Protestant Reformation, 3, 16–20

Puerto Rican Baptist Convention, 71

Rah, Soong-Chan, xi, xviii, 70, 93–99

Rice, Luther, 64, 67, 104, 109, 112

Richards, James, 66–67

Robert, Dana, 126

Ross, H. Miriam, 129

Roxburgh, William, 39

Roy, Rammohan, 42–59

Ryland, John, Jr., 111, 127

Ryland, John, Sr., 114–15

Saker, Alfred, 72

Sanneh, Lamin, 80

Sati, 4, 39–40, 42, 45

Schleiermacher, Friedrich, 16

Sekal O Ekal (Basu), 27

Seminario Bíblico Latinoamericano, 70

Serampore College, 4, 39

Serampore Trio, 43–44, 103, 123

Serious and Candid Letters (Worcester), 106

Seymour, William, 99

Shakespeare, William, 3

Sharpe, Henry, 94

Sharpe, Liele, 94

Sharpe, Nancy, 94

Short, Charles, 128

Shudra. *See* Caste.

Shwedagon Pagoda, 85–86, 89

Simeon, Charles, 8, 37

Smith, George, 3

Society of the Brethren, 77

South Sea, 19, 26

Southern Baptist Convention (SBC), 72, 114–19

Spurgeon, Charles, 4

Stennett I, Joseph, 108

Student Christian Movement (SCM), 68

Sutcliff, John, 8–10

Symes, Michael, 76

Tabernacle Church, 63–64, 77–78, 106

Taylor, Daniel, 13

Tennent, Timothy, xi, xvi, 15–26

Tertullian, 17

Thomas, John, 32–33, 121, 123

Tin, Pe Maung, 88–89

Transforming Mission (Bosch), 18

Treatise of Baptism (Danvers), 107

Triennial Convention, 103, 111, 132

Two Discourses (Worcester), 106

Udney, George, 36

Unitarianism, 12, 45

University of Halle, 16

Urbana, 68

Vaishya. *See* Caste.

Vedas. *See* Hinduism

View of the Economy (Austin), 106

Walker, Frank Deaville, 31

Walls, Andrew, 5, 80

Ward, William, 103, 105, 111, 123, 131

Warneck, Gustav, 16
Wayland, Francis, 108
Whitefield, George, 13
Wilberforce, William, 32
Williams, John, 109
Williams College, 66
Wills, Elizabeth, 30
Winona Lake School of Theology, 65
Winter, Ralph, 24
Winward Road Chapel, 95
Wood, Charles, 21
Worcester, Samuel, 77, 105–7
World Christian Encyclopedia, 10

World Missionary Conference (1910),
    24, 67
WuDunn, Sheryl, 83
Wycliffe, John, 4

Yeh, Allen, xi, xvii, 63–73
YMCA, 67
Yonge, C.M., 126

Zadda, Chakravarthy, xi, xvi, 27–41
Zayat, 70, 86, 89, 91
Ziegenbalg, Bartholomew, 18, 26
Zinzendorf, Nicolas von, 26

Printed in the USA
CPSIA information can be obtained
at www.ICGtesting.com
LVHW011925251123
764906LV00005B/122